Homemade Healthy Dog Food Cookbook

Make Your Furry Friend Live Healthier & Longer with 130 Easy and Scrumptious Recipes for a Balanced Diet, Healthy Treats, and 28-Day Transition Meal Plan

Vivian Gross

Table of contents

About the Author: Vivian Gross..**6**

Introduction **7**

Chapter 1: The Importance of Homemade Dog Food **9**

    1.1. The Benefits of a Homemade Balanced Diet for Dogs.........................9

    1.2. Drawbacks and Risks of Commercial Dog Food..................................9

    1.3. Understanding Canine Nutritional Needs 9

    1.4. Strengthening the Emotional Bond through Personalized Feeding............10

Chapter 2: Understanding the Need for Change...**11**

    2.1 The Pitfalls of Commercial Dog Food...11

    2.2 A Shift in Perspective: Back to Basics 11

    2.3 Health Considerations...11

    2.4 Behavioral Cues...12

    2.5 External Factors 12

    2.6 The Benefits of Homemade Dog Food 12

    2.7 A Journey Towards Healthier Feeding...13

Chapter 3: Canine Nutrition Basics..**14**

    3.1 The Main Food Parts: Proteins, Carbs, and Fats.................................14

        3.1.1 Proteins..14

        3.1.2 Carbohydrates (Carbs) 14

        3.1.3 Fats 14

    3.2. Important Vitamins and Minerals...15

        3.2.1 Vitamins...15

        3.2.2 Minerals 15

    3.3 Determining Food Amounts Based on Size, Age, and Activity 15

        3.3.1 Size..15

        3.3.2 Age 16

        3.3.3 Activity Level 16

Chapter 4: Safe Ingredients vs. Toxic Foods...**17**

    4.1 Comprehensive list of safe ingredients for dogs.................................17

    4.2 Detailed list of toxic or harmful foods for dogs and reasons.............17

    4.3 The gray areas..18

Chapter 5: Cooking conversion chart...**19**

Chapter 6: Balanced Diet Recipes...**20**

    6.1 Poultry-based dishes 20

        Herbed Chicken & Quinoa 20

Savory Turkey & Lentils..20

Chicken & Pumpkin Soup...21

Chicken, Brown Rice & Veggies..21

Turkey, Barley, and Green Beans Medley...22

Poultry Delight with Chickpeas and Kale...22

Chicken & Sweet Potato Stew..23

Ground Turkey & Cauliflower Rice...23

Duck & Barley Bowl...24

Turkey Liver & Brown Rice...24

Chicken Heart & Beet Medley..25

Ground Chicken & Spinach Pasta...25

Chicken, Broccoli, and Millet Feast..26

Ground Turkey & Sweet Pea Muffins..26

Chicken Heart & Rice Delight...27

Chicken and Rice Blend...27

Turkey and Barley Stew...28

Egg and Sweet Potato Scramble..28

6.2 Fish-centric recipes 29

Herring & Broccoli Bliss..29

Mackerel & Pumpkin Pie...29

Sardine & Spinach Mix..30

Tilapia & Sweet Pea Treat...30

Cod & Beet Medley..31

Trout & Apple Salad..31

Catfish & Veggie Stir-Fry...32

Flounder & Berry Mix..32

Salmon & Green Bean Delight...33

Tuna & Sweet Potato Mash...33

Whitefish & Cauliflower Rice...34

Mackerel & Spinach Stew..34

Sardine & Carrot Pasta...35

Haddock & Butternut Bowl..35

Prawn & Lentil Feast...36

Sole & Asparagus Blend..36

Cod & Pumpkin Puree...37

Tilapia & Beet Salad...37

Fish and Greens..38

Salmon and Lentil Delight...38

6.3 Red meat dishes 39

Beef & Vegetable Medley..39

Pork & Pea Casserole..39

Beef & Blueberry Muffins...40

Lamb & Lentil Mix..40

Beef Liver & Sweet Potato Mash..41

Classic Beef & Rice..41

Pork & Pumpkin Medley...42

Meaty Mutton & Potato Mash..42

Beef & Blueberry Fusion..43

Pork & Apple Delight...43

Beef Liver & Veggie Mix...44

Lamb & Pumpkin Stew...44

Beef & Green Bean Casserole...45

Beef Heart & Vegetable Stir-fry..45

Ground Beef & Broccoli Pie..46

Pork and Vegetable Blend..46

Lamb and Carrot Stew..47

Beef and Quinoa Mix..47

6.4 Vegetarian options...48

Chickpea & Spinach Stew...48

Rice & Veggies Medley..48

Sweet Potato & Tofu Delight..49

Quinoa & Veggie Bowl..49

Rice & Lentil Fusion...50

Cauliflower & Chia Seed Mix..50

Carrot & Bean Casserole..51

Pumpkin & Tempeh Treat...51

Broccoli & Cottage Cheese Platter..52

Beet & Brown Rice Bowl...52

Parsnip & Lentil Medley...53

Potato & Green Bean Blend..53

Oats & Vegetable Pottage...54

Buckwheat & Red Bell Pepper Chow..54

Chapter 7: Healthy Treats and Snacks..55

7.1 Biscuits and cookies...55

Peanut Butter Banana Bites...55

Pumpkin Carrot Sticks...55

Coconut Apple Rings..56

Sweet Potato Chews...56

Chicken & Parsley Biscuits...57

Berry Bone Biscuits..57

Oat & Honey Cookies 58

Beef & Veggie Medley 58

Peanut Crunch Bars 59

Salmon Squares 59

Cheese & Apple Balls 60

Tuna & Parsley Bites 60

Veggie & Quinoa Puffs 61

Lamb & Mint Cookies 61

Blueberry & Yogurt Drops 62

Spinach & Cheese Muffins 62

Chicken & Rice Cakes 63

Turkey & Cranberry Treats 63

Broccoli & Beef Nuggets 64

Quinoa & Carrot Sticks 64

7.2 Dehydrated and jerky treats 65

Peanut & Honey Jerky 65

Peanut Butter Banana Jerky 65

Beefy Bites 66

Dehydrated Veggie Medley 66

Chicken & Parsley Chews 67

Salmon Slivers 67

Oat & Apple Crunchies 68

Turmeric & Chicken Jerky 68

Pumpkin Pie Bites 69

Tuna Flakes 69

Coconut & Blueberry Bliss 70

Turkey & Cranberry Jerky 70

Beet & Carrot Twists 71

Berry Delight Chewy Strips 71

7.3 Cold treats for hot days 72

Peanut Butter & Banana Popsicles 72

Berry & Yogurt Ice Cubes 72

Coconut & Pineapple Chunks 73

Apple & Carrot Slush 73

Minty Fresh Breath Cubes 74

Watermelon & Coconut Coolers 74

Mango & Ginger Freeze 75

Peanut & Honey Drops 75

Berry & Chia Pops 76

Green Tea & Apple Cubes 76

7.4 Chewy delights 77

    Sweet Potato Chews 77

    Peanut Butter & Oat Bars 77

    Chicken Jerky Strips 78

    Beef & Carrot Sticks 78

    Salmon & Parsley Bites 79

    Apple & Cinnamon Rolls 79

    Banana & Coconut Chewies 80

    Blueberry & Almond Bars 80

    Pumpkin & Flaxseed Twists 81

    Spinach & Carrot Sticks 81

Chapter 8: The Importance of Hydration **82**

8.1 Understanding Dogs' Hydration Needs Across Seasons 82

8.2 Flavorful Broth Recipes for Hydration 82

    Chicken & Carrot Broth 82

    Vegetable Hydration Broth 83

    Beef & Parsley Broth 83

    Turkey & Sweet Potato Broth 84

    Fish & Pea Broth 84

8.3 Tips on Ensuring Your Dog is Drinking Enough 85

Chapter 9: The Importance of Gradual Transitions **86**

Chapter 10: 28-Day Transition Meal Plan **87**

Week 1: The Gentle Introduction 87

Week 2: Balancing Act 87

Week 3: Tipping the Scales 88

Week 4: The Complete Transition 88

Conclusion **89**

About the Author: Vivian Gross

In the world of canine wellness and culinary expertise, Vivian Gross stands as a beacon for all dog enthusiasts. Author of the "Homemade Healthy Dog Food Cookbook: Make Your Furry Friend Live Healthier & Longer with 130 Easy and Scrumptious Recipes for a Balanced Diet, Healthy Treats, and 28-Day Transition Meal Plan," Vivian's journey began not from the confines of a kitchen, but from a lifetime spent communicating and bonding with dogs of every conceivable breed. Her innate understanding of these loyal companions stems from a profound love and respect, combined with an unwavering commitment to enhancing the quality and longevity of their lives.

From a very young age, Vivian recognized the unique bond that humans share with their dogs. Rather than merely seeing them as pets, she observed them as family members, deserving of care, attention, and above all, a healthy diet that matches the richness of their spirit. As years passed, this realization transformed into a mission: to equip fellow dog lovers with the knowledge and recipes that would ensure their furry friends thrived.

Living her philosophy daily, Vivian shares her life with four beloved dogs, each a testament to her commitment and expertise. Their radiant health and spirited playfulness bear witness to the benefits of a wholesome, homemade diet. As she continues to create and innovate in her kitchen, Vivian's dogs serve both as her inspiration and as the most genuine reviewers of her culinary creations. Their wagging tails and eager eyes are the best endorsement for the recipes found within her book, assuring readers that the dishes are not just nutritious but irresistibly delicious.

In "Homemade Healthy Dog Food Cookbook: Make Your Furry Friend Live Healthier & Longer with 130 Easy and Scrumptious Recipes for a Balanced Diet, Healthy Treats, and 28-Day Transition Meal Plan," readers are not merely presented with a collection of recipes. They're invited into Vivian's world, where every dish is a product of meticulous research, passionate cooking, and real-world experience with her canine companions. The book promises more than just meals—it offers a holistic approach to dog nutrition, encompassing everything from balanced diets to healthy treats, and even a carefully crafted 28-Day Transition Meal Plan.

Vivian Gross is more than an author; she's an advocate for canine health, a culinary innovator in the world of pet food, and most importantly, a trusted friend to every reader and their furry family member.

Dive into the world Vivian has crafted, and let her guide you to a happier, healthier life for your own canine companions.

Introduction

The Bond Between Dogs and Humans

From the moment our ancestors tamed the first wolves, forging a bond based on mutual benefit, to today's modern households, where dogs are treasured members of the family, our relationship with these wonderful creatures has continued to evolve. Dogs have not just been man's best friend but have also been guardians, shepherds, hunters, and loyal companions. The deep connection we share with our furry friends **is one of love, trust, and mutual respect.**

However, with this bond comes a significant responsibility. As guardians of their well-being, it falls upon us to ensure they lead happy, healthy, and fulfilling lives. A pivotal component **of this is their diet**, which plays an essential role in determining their overall health, longevity, and vitality.

The Problems with Commercial Dog Foods

In today's fast-paced world, many pet owners turn to commercial dog foods as a convenient solution. At a glance, these products seem to offer complete nutrition tailored to our pets' needs. Yet, a closer look reveals a more troubling picture.

Many commercial dog foods, especially the cheaper varieties, are packed with fillers, artificial additives, preservatives, and low-quality ingredients that can be detrimental to our dogs' health. Some have been linked to allergies, digestive issues, obesity, and other chronic health problems. The frequent recalls due to contamination or unsafe ingredients further erode the trust in these products.

Moreover, just as humans thrive best on a varied diet, our dogs to deserve a range of wholesome foods that cater to their specific nutritional requirements, rather than a one-size-fits-all approach.

The Mission of This Book

"Homemade Healthy Dog Food Cookbook: Make Your Furry Friend Live Healthier & Longer with 130 Easy and Scrumptious Recipes for a Balanced Diet, Healthy Treats, and 28-Day Transition Meal Plan" was born out of a simple yet profound idea: **Our dogs deserve the best.** This book isn't just a collection of recipes; it's a testament to our commitment to providing our dogs with the best possible nutrition.

Wholesome Dog Food: Why Homemade?

A homemade balanced diet for dogs goes beyond just filling their bellies. It means feeding them with food that supports their overall health, vitality, and longevity. Benefits of such a diet include:

- Optimal Weight Management: Homemade foods, when done right, can prevent obesity, ensuring your dog maintains an ideal weight.
- Increased Energy and Vitality: A proper diet can rev up your dog's energy, giving them the zest to play and live fully.
- Better Skin and Coat Health: Say goodbye to dull fur and skin issues. The right nutrients can lead to a shiny coat and healthier skin.

- Improved Digestive Health: Homemade meals can be easier for dogs to digest, leading to fewer gastrointestinal problems.
- Reduced Allergies: By knowing every ingredient that goes into your dog's meal, you can avoid allergens that may cause reactions.

The Journey Towards Longer, Healthier Life for Your Furry Friend

Every pet owner dreams of sharing many joyful years with their furry friend. The journey to longer, healthier life starts with every bite. By choosing homemade meals, you're not just giving them food; you're giving them life. This cookbook provides recipes that are not only delicious but also balanced and nutritious, ensuring that every mealtime is a step towards longevity and health.

The Importance of Gradual Transitions

While the allure of diving straight into these scrumptious recipes is hard to resist, it's crucial to remember that any dietary change should be made gradually. Dogs have sensitive stomachs, and a sudden shift can cause digestive upsets. **The 28-Day Transition Meal Plan** included in this cookbook ensures a smooth and comfortable shift from processed foods to these homemade delights. By following it, you'll ensure that your dog doesn't just enjoy the new meals, but thrives on them.

Within these pages, you'll discover **130 easy and scrumptious recipes tailored for a balanced diet.** These meals are crafted with love, prioritizing fresh, whole ingredients, and avoiding the pitfalls of many commercial dog foods. Moreover, you'll find **delightful treats** that will make your dog's tail wag in joy and a comprehensive 28-day transition meal plan to shift your furry friend to a homemade diet gently and safely.

Our mission is clear: to empower you with the knowledge and tools to provide a healthier, more balanced diet for your beloved pet. Because at the end of the day, when we make meals with our own hands, infused with love and the best ingredients, we don't just feed their bodies; we also nourish their souls.

So, grab your apron and let's embark on this delightful culinary journey for our furry friends, ensuring they live healthier, longer, and happier lives by our side.

Chapter 1: The Importance of Homemade Dog Food

In an era where health consciousness is paramount, many dog owners are taking the initiative to ensure their pets are also eating well. Gone are the days of feeding pets whatever's handy; today, we recognize that dogs have distinct dietary needs. While the convenience of commercial dog food is tempting, there's a lot to be said for homemade dog food.

1.1. The Benefits of a Homemade Balanced Diet for Dogs

Quality Assurance: When you prepare your dog's meal, you have full control over the quality of ingredients used. There's no second-guessing about the freshness of the produce or the authenticity of the meat sources. This transparency is the cornerstone of trust in food quality.

Tailored Nutrition: No two dogs are identical in their nutritional needs. By preparing meals at home, you can tailor the food according to your pet's specific requirements, taking into account age, weight, activity level, and health conditions.

Diverse Ingredients: A homemade diet offers variety, which means a broader range of nutrients. While a commercial food might focus on a single protein source, at home, you can mix and match, ensuring a well-rounded intake.

Avoidance of Allergens: If your dog is allergic or sensitive to specific ingredients commonly found in commercial foods, a homemade diet allows you to eliminate or substitute these components easily.

1.2. Drawbacks and Risks of Commercial Dog Food

Mystery Ingredients: Many commercial dog foods, even those labeled "premium," contain fillers, by-products, and meat meals, the exact origins of which remain uncertain.

Preservatives and Chemicals: Chemical preservatives, artificial colors, and flavors are rampant in many dog foods, which can lead to long-term health complications and immediate allergic reactions in some pets.

Recall Risks: Over the years, numerous brands have recalled their products due to contamination. Homemade food eliminates the risk of mass-produced contamination.

Lack of Freshness: Stored for an indefinite time, commercial dog food lacks the freshness that a newly prepared meal can offer. Even with preservation methods, vital nutrients can degrade over time.

1.3. Understanding Canine Nutritional Needs

Proteins: Essential for every cellular function, proteins are the building blocks of life. A dog's diet should be rich in high-quality proteins from sources like chicken, beef, fish, and lamb.

Fats: Fats provide energy and are essential for brain development, especially in puppies. Omega fatty acids found in fish oils, flaxseed, and certain animal fats are vital for skin health and coat shine.

Carbohydrates: Often maligned, but essential, carbohydrates provide quick energy. Opt for complex carbs like sweet potatoes, brown rice, and barley for sustained energy and digestive health.

Vitamins and Minerals: These micronutrients, though required in small amounts, play vital roles in processes from bone development to nerve function. They're found in vegetables, fruits, meats, and specially formulated supplements.

Water: Dehydration can lead to severe complications. Always ensure your dog has access to clean, fresh water.

1.4. Strengthening the Emotional Bond through Personalized Feeding

Cooking as an Act of Love: The time and effort you invest in preparing your dog's meal translate to care, strengthening the bond between you and your pet. Dogs, with their keen senses, can recognize this act of love.

Recognizing Preferences: Observing what your dog likes or dislikes in homemade meals can lead to a deeper understanding of their personalities and preferences.

Trust and Reliability: When dogs get a consistent diet that's both tasty and makes them feel good, it enhances trust. They begin to view you as not just their owner but their protector, ensuring they receive the best.

Mealtime as a Ritual: With homemade food, mealtimes become more than just eating. It's a ritual, an opportunity for interaction, training, and mutual respect.

In conclusion, while the debate on homemade vs. commercial dog food continues, what remains undisputed is the intention behind the choice. By understanding the importance of a balanced diet, recognizing the pitfalls of commercial options, and realizing the bond that personalized feeding can forge, dog owners can make informed choices for their beloved pets. Your journey through this book will provide further insights and tools to make this choice a rewarding one for both you and your canine companion.

Chapter 2: Understanding the Need for Change

In the world of pet care, it's easy to settle into familiar routines. We often feed our dogs the same food day after day, mostly because it's convenient. However, the evolving understanding of canine nutrition and health suggests that a change might be necessary. The pet feed industry has changed significantly in the last few decades.

The surge in demand for commercial dog food has led to the mass production of foods that are not always of the highest quality. While convenience is a boon for busy pet owners, the true nutritional value of these foods has come into question.

Let's delve into the various reasons that may compel you to consider homemade healthy dog food.

2.1 The Pitfalls of Commercial Dog Food

Questionable Ingredients: One of the primary concerns pet owners have with commercial dog food is the use of subpar ingredients. Some contain fillers like corn and wheat gluten, which offer little to no nutritional value. Others may contain animal by-products, which can be anything from organs to bones, often not the choice parts of an animal.

Additives and Preservatives: Many commercial foods have additives, dyes, and preservatives that can lead to allergic reactions and other health issues in dogs. Artificial flavors and colors don't contribute to a dog's health and can be harmful over time.

Misleading Advertising: The vibrant pictures of fresh meat, veggies, and grains on pet food bags can be misleading. The actual product inside might not be as fresh or wholesome as the packaging suggests.

2.2 A Shift in Perspective: Back to Basics

Historically, dogs thrived on diets consisting of fresh meats, bones, and some fruits and vegetables they foraged or scavenged. This natural diet, free from chemicals and artificial substances, was rich in nutrients and contributed to their overall health and vitality.

With the rise in health problems among dogs, such as obesity, diabetes, and allergies, many experts and veterinarians are now pointing at diet as a potential cause. This revelation has triggered a pressing need for change, leading many pet owners to consider alternative, healthier feeding options.

2.3 Health Considerations

Allergies: A sneeze here, a rash there, and suddenly your vibrant pup seems sluggish and in discomfort. Allergies in dogs are more common than we think, and often, the commercial foods we provide are the culprits. These foods might contain fillers, artificial colors, and flavor enhancers that might not agree with all dogs. A shift to homemade meals allows for a cleaner, allergen-free diet. By understanding and eliminating allergenic ingredients, you pave the way for a life free from these avoidable discomforts.

Nutritional Needs Across Life Stages: As dogs transition from playful puppies to mature seniors, their dietary needs change. While there are specialized commercial options available for different life stages, a homemade diet offers a unique level of adaptability. For instance, older dogs might require meals that are gentle on their joints, whereas young pups need calcium-enriched foods to support their rapidly growing bones.

Medical Conditions: Canine health can be a complex landscape. Conditions like diabetes or kidney issues necessitate a particular diet. Relying on off-the-shelf food might not always suffice. With homemade meals, every ingredient can be chosen with care, ensuring that your dog's specific medical condition is kept in check.

2.4 Behavioral Cues

Preferences and Dislikes: Just as we have our food favorites, our furry friends do too. Sometimes, it's not about health but pure taste. If your dog hesitates or outright refuses to eat certain commercial foods, it could be a sign. By switching to homemade meals, you have the flexibility to include their favorites and exclude what they detest.

Digestive Red Flags: Constant digestive issues can be distressing for both the dog and the owner. Loose stools, frequent vomiting, or gassiness can sometimes trace back to the commercial food's ingredients. Preparing meals at home gives you control over what goes into the bowl, ensuring that it aligns with your dog's digestive harmony.

2.5 External Factors

Availability: We don't all live in places where high-quality dog food is readily available. Sometimes, what's accessible might not meet our or our pet's standards. By preparing meals at home, you can ensure quality and make the best use of what's locally available, even if it means deviating from conventional dog food ingredients.

Budget-Friendly Choices: Top-tier commercial dog foods come with a hefty price tag. For many, this can stretch the monthly budget thin. Preparing dog meals at home can be a budget-friendly alternative. By buying ingredients in bulk or on sale and by focusing on seasonal produce, one can achieve significant savings without compromising on quality.

Seasonal Variety: Mother Nature offers a diverse palate. By aligning your dog's diet with the seasons, you introduce a delightful variety. This can be both nutritionally beneficial and a source of excitement for your dog. Winter might see more root vegetables, while summer can bring in fresh berries and leafy greens.

2.6 The Benefits of Homemade Dog Food

Transparency and Control: When you prepare your dog's meals at home, you know exactly what goes into them. You can choose high-quality, fresh ingredients and tailor the diet according to your dog's specific needs.

Nutrient-rich Meals: Homemade food ensures that your pet gets a balanced meal with proteins, carbs, fats, vitamins, and minerals. You have the power to add or exclude any ingredient.

Avoiding Allergens: If your dog is allergic to certain food items, you can easily avoid them. On the other hand, finding commercial dog food that doesn't contain common allergens can be a challenging task.

Building a Stronger Bond: Preparing meals for your dog can also serve as a bonding activity. Watching your pet enjoy a meal you've made is immensely satisfying.

2.7 A Journey Towards Healthier Feeding

Understanding the need for change is the first step in a journey toward healthier feeding habits for our canine companions. As we delve deeper into the nuances of dog nutrition in the following chapters, you'll be equipped with knowledge and recipes to make meals that are both delicious and nutritious.

The love we have for our dogs demands nothing but the best for them. Changing their diet to a healthier, homemade option is a labor of love, one that promises a happier, more vibrant life for our furry friends. Stay tuned as the next chapter guides you on the basics of canine nutrition and the building blocks of a balanced homemade dog meal.

Chapter 3: Canine Nutrition Basics

Understanding your dog's nutrition is crucial for their health. This chapter simplifies the core components of a dog's diet and how to determine the right food amounts.

3.1 The Main Food Parts: Proteins, Carbs, and Fats

3.1.1 Proteins

Role: Proteins play a foundational role in the health and maintenance of a dog's body. They are the primary building blocks for tissues, organs, enzymes, hormones, and antibodies. Additionally, they're responsible for growth in younger animals and for repairing worn-out or damaged tissues in older animals.
Sources:
- Meats: This includes a range of options from poultry (chicken, turkey) to red meats (beef, lamb) and even game meats.
- Fish: Oily fish like salmon provides both protein and beneficial omega-3 fatty acids.
- Eggs: They're not just a protein powerhouse but also contain essential vitamins and minerals.

Daily Amount: Protein requirements can vary based on several factors. Puppies, pregnant dogs, and active breeds might require more protein. Generally, adult dogs should have between 18-25% protein in their diet, while puppies might need up to 28%.

3.1.2 Carbohydrates (Carbs)

Role: Carbohydrates serve as a primary source of quick energy for dogs. They provide glucose, which can be used immediately or stored in the liver and muscles for later use. Furthermore, they aid in the digestion and absorption of other nutrients.
Sources:
- Whole Grains: Brown rice, barley, and oats are excellent grains that provide sustained energy.
- Vegetables: Sweet potatoes, carrots, and peas are not only sources of carbs but also offer vitamins and fiber.
- Fruits: While they can be a source of carbs, it's essential to give fruits in moderation and ensure they are safe for canine consumption.

Daily Amount: While dogs don't have a biological need for carbohydrates, they can be beneficial, especially for active dogs. Depending on a dog's activity level and metabolism, carbs can make up anywhere from 30-70% of their diet. However, a general range is around 50-55%.

3.1.3 Fats

Role: Fats are more than just an energy reserve; they are crucial for brain development, absorption of specific vitamins (like A, D, E, and K), and maintaining healthy skin and coat. They also act as carriers for essential fatty acids.
Sources:
- Animal Fats: This includes fats derived from meats that dogs consume.
- Oils: Fish oil is renowned for its omega-3 fatty acid content. Other beneficial oils include flaxseed oil and olive oil.

Daily Amount: Fats are energy-dense, providing more than double the energy of proteins or carbs per gram. Depending on a dog's size, age, and activity level, fats should generally constitute about 25-30% of their diet.

3.2. Important Vitamins and Minerals

3.2.1 Vitamins

- Vitamin A: Important for vision. Found in liver and fish oils.
- Vitamin D: Crucial for bone health. Found in sunlight and fish oils.
- B Vitamins: Boost energy. Found in meats and grains.
- Daily Amount: Specific requirements vary, but commercial dog foods usually have the recommended dose.

3.2.2 Minerals

- Calcium & Phosphorus: For bone health. Found in bones and dairy. Dogs should get about 0.5-0.8% calcium and 0.4-0.7% phosphorus in their diet.
- Iron: Helps in oxygen transport. Found in meats and spinach. The recommendation is about 80 mg/kg of a dog's diet.

3.3 Determining Food Amounts Based on Size, Age, and Activity

3.3.1 Size

Dogs of different sizes have varying metabolic rates, which means their caloric needs can be vastly different:

- Toy Breeds (up to 12 lbs):
  - ✓ They often have a faster metabolism, requiring around 40 calories per pound of body weight.
  - ✓ Example: A 10 lb Chihuahua would need approximately 400 calories/day.

- Small to Medium Breeds (12-50 lbs):
  - ✓ Generally require around 30-35 calories per pound of body weight.
  - ✓ Example: A 30 lb Beagle might need around 900 to 1050 calories/day.

- Large Breeds (50-100 lbs):
  - ✓ Their metabolic rate is slower, requiring around 20-25 calories per pound.
  - ✓ Example: An 80 lb Labrador might need 1600 to 2000 calories/day.

- Giant Breeds (over 100 lbs):
  - ✓ Need around 18-20 calories per pound, given their slower metabolism.
  - ✓ Example: A 120 lb Great Dane might need around 2160 to 2400 calories/day.

3.3.2 Age

Dogs at different life stages have different caloric needs:
- Puppies:
    - ✓ Require more calories to support their rapid growth and high energy levels. Depending on their size, they may need 50-100% more calories than their adult counterparts.
- Adults:
    - ✓ Caloric needs stabilize during adulthood. Follow size-based guidelines, adjusting for activity.
- Seniors:
    - ✓ As they become less active and their metabolism slows, they might need 20% fewer calories than younger adults. It's also essential to monitor their weight and health regularly.

3.3.3 Activity Level

The amount of exercise and activity your dog gets can significantly influence their caloric needs:
- Sedentary:
    - ✓ Dogs that are less active or elderly might need fewer calories. Reduce the general guideline by 10-20%.
- Moderately Active:
    - ✓ Dogs that get regular walks and play sessions but aren't overly active should stick to the general caloric guidelines for their size and age.
- Highly Active:
    - ✓ Working dogs, athletes, or those that get intensive training/exercise sessions might need 20-40% more calories than the standard recommendation.

Chapter 4: Safe Ingredients vs. Toxic Foods

4.1 Comprehensive list of safe ingredients for dogs

Homemade dog food can be a delightful treat for your canine friend when done right. Knowing which ingredients are safe for dogs can ensure they get the nutrients they need without any harmful side effects.

- **Meats:** Lean meats such as chicken, turkey, beef, lamb, pork and duck. Always cook these to kill off harmful bacteria.
- **Fish:** Like salmon and tuna, which are excellent sources of Omega-3 fatty acids. Sardines: Rich in omega-3 fatty acids and can be given occasionally. Mackerel: Another good fish option, rich in essential oils and nutrients. Whitefish: A digestible fish for dogs, but ensure it's boneless.
- **Vegetables:** Carrots, green beans, peas, spinach, cucumbers, and Brussels sprouts.
  Broccoli: In small amounts, as it can cause digestive upset in large quantities.
  Sweet potatoes: A great source of dietary fiber, vitamins B6 and C, beta carotene, and manganese.
  Pumpkin: Good for digestion and can help with diarrhea and constipation.
  Zucchini: Low in calories and a good source of dietary fiber.
  Kale: Packed with vitamins and minerals, but best given in moderation.
  Cabbage: This can help with digestion but should be given in moderation to avoid gas.
- **Fruits:**
  Blueberries, strawberries, apples (without seeds or core), and watermelon (seedless).
  Bananas: High in potassium and vitamins C and B6.
  Cranberries: Good for urinary tract health, but should be unsweetened.
  Pears: Make sure to remove the seeds and core.
  Oranges: Remove the seeds and peel, and offer in moderation due to sugar content.
  Pineapple: A natural meat tenderizer and rich in vitamins and minerals.
- **Grains:**
  Rice (brown or white), quinoa, and oatmeal.
  Barley: This can be easily digested and is good for the heart.
  Lentils: A good source of iron, protein, and fiber.
  Chickpeas: Rich in protein and fiber but should be given in moderation.
  Pearled millet: Gluten-free, alkaline grain, making it easy to digest.
- **Dairy (in moderation):** Low-fat yogurt and cottage cheese.
- **Eggs:** Fully cooked.
- **Oils:** Fish oil, coconut oil, and olive oil (in moderation).
- **Flaxseed:** A source of omega-3 fatty acids. It can be ground up and added to dog food.
- **Turmeric:** Has anti-inflammatory properties, but introduce slowly and in small amounts.
- **Seaweed:** A source of essential vitamins and minerals.

4.2 Detailed list of toxic or harmful foods for dogs and reasons

Many common foods, safe for humans, can be toxic to dogs. It's vital to be aware of these and avoid including them in any homemade recipes:

- Chocolate: Contains theobromine, which is toxic to dogs.
- Onions and Garlic: These can cause gastrointestinal irritation and lead to red blood cell damage.

- Grapes and Raisins: The exact cause is unknown, but they can cause kidney failure in dogs.
- Macadamia Nuts: Can cause weakness, vomiting, tremors, and hyperthermia.
- Alcohol: Causes vomiting, disorientation, and, in severe cases, death.
- Coffee and Caffeine: Can lead to restlessness, rapid breathing, and heart palpitations.
- Xylitol (found in sugar-free gums and candies): Causes insulin release leading to liver failure.
- Avocado: Contains persin, which can cause diarrhea, vomiting, and heart congestion.
- Bones: Can splinter and cause obstructions or tears in the digestive system.
- Fruit seeds and pits: Some, like apple seeds, contain trace amounts of cyanide.

4.3 The gray areas

Controversial ingredients and when to be cautious:
- Raw diets: While some dog owners swear by raw diets, feeding raw meat can pose risks of bacterial infections such as salmonella. If considering this, do thorough research and consult with a veterinarian.
- Dairy: Some dogs are lactose intolerant. While small amounts of certain dairy products might be okay, they can cause digestive upset in some dogs.
- Grains: While many dogs digest grains without issue, some dog owners believe grains can lead to allergies or other health issues. It's essential to watch for any signs of allergies or intolerances.
- Tomatoes: While ripe tomatoes are generally considered safe, green parts of the tomato plant are toxic.

Always consult a veterinarian before introducing a new ingredient into your dog's diet or making significant changes to their meals. They can provide guidance tailored to your dog's specific needs.

KITCHEN CONVERSIONS CHART

how to easily convert units of measurements

1 GALLON	1 QUART	1 PINT	1 CUP	1 OUNCE	1 TBSP	1 TSP
4 QUARTS 8 PINTS 16 CUPS 128 OUNCES 3,8 LITERS	2 PINTS 4 CUPS 32 OUNCES 950 ML	2 CUPS 16 OUNCES 480 ML	16 TBSP 8 OUNCES 240 ML	2 TBSP 30 ML	3 TSP 1/2 OUNCES 15 ML	5 ML

1 gallon = 4 quarts, 8 pints, 16 cups, 128 ounces and 3.8 liters
1 quart = 2 pints, 4 cups, 32 ounces and 950 ml
1 pint = 2 cups, 16 ounces and 480 ml
1 cup = 16 tablespoons, 8 ounces and 240 ml
1 ounce = 2 tablespoons and 30 ml
1 tablespoon = 3 teaspoons, 1/2 ounce and 15 ml
1 teaspoon = 5 ml

1 teaspoon = 5 ml
1 tablespoon = 3 teaspoons = 15 ml
2 tablespoons = 1 ounce = 30 ml
4 tablespoons = 1/4 cup = 60 ml
5 tablespoons + 1 teaspoon = 1/3 cup = 80 ml
1/2 cup = 8 tablespoons = 120 ml
1 cup = 16 tablespoons = 240 ml
1 quart = 2 pints = 4 cups
1 gallon = 4 quarts = 16 cups
1 stick butter = 8 tablespoons = 1/2 cup = 4 ounces = 113 grams

Chapter 6: Balanced Diet Recipes

6.1 Poultry-based dishes

Herbed Chicken & Quinoa

Yield: 4 servings | Prep time: 10 minutes | Cook time: 25 minutes

Age: Adult dogs & Puppies (6 to 12 months)

Weight per serving: Suitable for Medium breeds (20-50 lbs

Ingredients:

- 2 boneless chicken breasts
- 1 cup cooked quinoa
- 1/2 cup chopped spinach
- 1 tsp dried oregano
- 1 tbsp olive oil

Directions:

1. Grill or boil the chicken until fully cooked, then dice.
2. In a bowl, mix the cooked quinoa and chopped spinach.
3. Sprinkle dried oregano and mix well.
4. Drizzle with olive oil and stir to combine before serving.

Nutritional Information (approx. per serving): 280 calories, 24g protein, 20g carbohydrates, 9g fat

Savory Turkey & Lentils

Yield: 3 servings | Prep time: 10 minutes | Cook time: 20 minutes

Age: Puppies (4 to 12 months) & Adult dogs

Weight per serving: Suitable for Small breeds (10-20 lbs)

Ingredients:

- 1 pound ground turkey
- 1/2 cup cooked lentils
- 1/2 cup diced zucchini
- 1 tbsp flaxseed oil

Directions:

1. Cook ground turkey in a pan until browned.
2. Mix in the cooked lentils and diced zucchini.
3. Cook for an additional 5 minutes on low heat.
4. Remove from heat, let cool, then drizzle with flaxseed oil and serve.

Nutritional Information (approx. per serving): 310 calories, 30g protein, 18g carbohydrates, 12g fat

🐾 Chicken & Pumpkin Soup

🍽 Yield: 4 servings | Prep time: 10 minutes | Cook time: 25 minutes

Age: Senior dogs & Puppies (8 to 12 months)

Weight per serving: Suitable for Medium breeds (20-50 lbs)

Ingredients:

- 2 boneless chicken thighs
- 1 cup pumpkin puree
- 1/2 cup green beans, chopped
- 2 cups chicken broth (low sodium)

Directions:

1. In a pot, cook chicken thighs with broth until fully done.
2. Add pumpkin puree and green beans.
3. Simmer for 10 minutes.
4. Let cool before serving.

Nutritional Information (approx. per serving): 210 calories, 20g protein, 15g carbohydrates, 8g fat

🐾 Chicken, Brown Rice & Veggies

🍽 Yield: 5 servings | Prep time: 15 minutes | Cook time: 35 minutes

Age: Adult dogs & Puppies (5 to 12 months)

Weight per serving: Suitable for Medium breeds (20-50 lbs)

Ingredients:

- 2 boneless, skinless chicken breasts
- 1 cup brown rice (cooked)
- 1/2 cup carrots, finely diced
- 1/2 cup peas
- 1/4 cup sweet potato, diced
- 1 tbsp fish oil (for Omega-3s)

Directions:

1. Boil the chicken breasts in a large pot until fully cooked. Once done, let them cool and then shred the meat.
2. In the same pot, with a small amount of the chicken water remaining, cook the carrots, peas, and sweet potato until they're soft.
3. Combine the shredded chicken, cooked brown rice, and the vegetables in a large bowl and mix well.
4. Drizzle the fish oil over the mixture for added health benefits.

Nutritional Information (approx. per serving): 320 calories, 26g protein, 30g carbohydrates, 9g fat

Turkey, Barley, and Green Beans Medley

Yield: 6 servings | Prep time: 15 minutes | Cook time: 40 minutes

Age: Adult dogs & Puppies (7 to 12 months)

Weight per serving: Suitable for Large breeds (50-100 lbs)

Ingredients:

- 1 pound ground turkey
- 1 cup barley (cooked)
- 1 cup green beans, chopped
- 1/2 cup broccoli, finely chopped
- 1/4 cup blueberries (for antioxidants)
- 1 tbsp coconut oil

Directions:

1. In a skillet over medium heat, cook the ground turkey until it's browned, breaking it into small pieces as it cooks.
2. In a separate pot, steam the green beans and broccoli until they're tender but still slightly crisp.
3. In a large mixing bowl, combine the cooked turkey, barley, green beans, broccoli, and blueberries.
4. Add the coconut oil and stir to combine.

Nutritional Information (approx. per serving): 350 calories, 28g protein, 32g carbohydrates, 12g fat

Poultry Delight with Chickpeas and Kale

Yield: 4 servings | Prep time: 15 minutes | Cook time: 30 minutes

Age: Adult dogs & Puppies (6 to 12 months)

Weight per serving: Suitable for Medium breeds (20-50 lbs)

Ingredients:

- 1 pound chicken thighs, boneless and skinless
- 1 cup chickpeas, cooked and mashed
- 1 cup kale, finely chopped
- 1/2 cup butternut squash, cubed
- 2 tbsp olive oil
- 1/4 tsp turmeric (for anti-inflammatory benefits)

Directions:

1. In a pot, boil chicken thighs until fully cooked. Once done, shred the meat.
2. Steam the butternut squash cubes until they're tender.
3. In a large bowl, combine the shredded chicken, mashed chickpeas, steamed squash, and finely chopped kale.
4. Add olive oil and turmeric, then mix

Nutritional Information (approx. per serving): 330 calories, 27g protein, 28g carbohydrates, 13g fat

Chicken & Sweet Potato Stew

Yield: 4 servings | Prep time: 15 minutes | Cook time: 30 minutes

Age: Senior dogs & Puppies (9 to 12 months)

Weight per serving: Suitable for Small breeds (10-20 lbs)

Ingredients:
- 1 pound chicken breast
- 1 large sweet potato, cubed
- 1/2 cup green peas
- 2 cups chicken broth (low sodium)
- 1 tbsp chia seeds

Directions:
1. Place chicken breasts and sweet potato cubes in a pot with chicken broth.
2. Simmer until chicken is cooked and sweet potatoes are tender.
3. Add green peas and cook for another 5 minutes.
4. Once cooled, shred the chicken and mix with chia seeds.
5. Serve when cooled to room temperature.

Nutritional Information (approx. per serving): 290 calories, 28g protein, 32g carbohydrates, 6g fat

Ground Turkey & Cauliflower Rice

Yeld: 3 servings | Prep time: 10 minutes | Cook time: 20 minutes

Age: Adult dogs

Weight per serving: Suitable for Medium breeds (20-50 lbs)

Ingredients:
- 1 pound ground turkey
- 1 cup cauliflower, riced
- 1/2 cup cooked lentils
- 1 tbsp coconut oil
- A pinch of parsley

Directions:
1. Brown the ground turkey in a pan until fully cooked.
2. Mix in the cauliflower rice and cook for another 5 minutes.
3. Stir in the lentils and cook for an additional 2 minutes.
4. Remove from heat, stir in coconut oil and sprinkle with parsley.

Nutritional Information (approx. per serving): 310 calories, 30g protein, 12g carbohydrates, 16g fat.

Duck & Barley Bowl

Yield: 4 servings | Prep time: 15 minutes | Cook time: 40 minutes

Age: Adult dogs & Puppies (8 to 12 months)

Weight per serving: Suitable for Large breeds (50-100 lbs) bs)

Ingredients:
- 2 duck breasts, skinned and deboned
- 1 cup barley
- 1/2 cup diced zucchini
- 1/2 cup pumpkin puree
- 2 cups water

Directions:
1. Cut duck breasts into small pieces and place in a pot with water.
2. Add barley and simmer until duck is cooked and barley is tender.
3. Mix in the zucchini and cook for another 10 minutes.
4. Once cooled, stir in the pumpkin puree.

Nutritional Information (approx. per serving): 370 calories, 34g protein, 35g carbohydrates, 9g fat.

Turkey Liver & Brown Rice

Yield: 4 servings | Prep time: 10 minutes | Cook time: 25 minutes

Age: Adult dogs

Weight per serving: Suitable for Medium breeds (20-50 lbs

Ingredients:
- 1 pound turkey liver, finely chopped
- 1 cup brown rice
- 1/4 cup finely chopped kale
- 1/4 cup cranberries (unsweetened)
- 1 tbsp olive oil

Directions:
1. Cook the brown rice according to the package directions.
2. In a separate pan, sauté turkey liver until fully cooked.
3. Mix liver, kale, and cranberries into the cooked rice.
4. Drizzle with olive oil before serving.

Nutritional Information (approx. per serving): 280 calories, 26g protein, 33g carbohydrates, 5g fat.

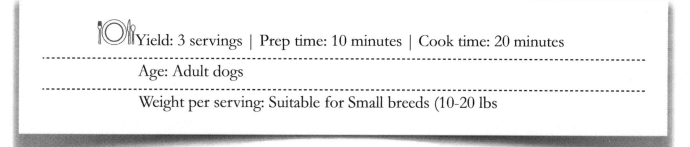

Chicken Heart & Beet Medley

Yield: 3 servings | **Prep time:** 10 minutes | **Cook time:** 20 minutes

Age: Adult dogs

Weight per serving: Suitable for Small breeds (10-20 lbs

Ingredients:

- 1 pound chicken hearts, halved
- 1/2 cup diced beets
- 1/2 cup quinoa, cooked
- 2 cups chicken broth (low sodium)
- 1 tbsp flaxseed

Directions:

1. In a pot, simmer chicken hearts and beets in chicken broth until hearts are fully cooked.
2. Drain excess liquid and mix in quinoa.
3. Sprinkle flaxseed on top before serving.

Nutritional Information (approx. per serving): 240 calories, 23g protein, 20g carbohydrates, 7g fat.

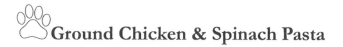

Ground Chicken & Spinach Pasta

Yield: 5 servings | **Prep time:** 15 minutes | **Cook time:** 30 minutes

Age: Adult dogs & Puppies (7 to 12 months)

Weight per serving: Suitable for Medium breeds (20-50 lbs)

Ingredients:

- 1 pound ground chicken
- 1/2 cup whole wheat pasta
- 1 cup spinach, finely chopped
- 1 tbsp fish oil
- 1/4 tsp ground turmeric

Directions:

1. Cook pasta as per package instructions and drain.
2. Brown the ground chicken in a pan.
3. Mix in spinach and cook until wilted.
4. Combine chicken mixture with pasta, drizzle with fish oil, and sprinkle with turmeric.

Nutritional Information (approx. per serving): 260 calories, 22g protein, 20g carbohydrates, 10g fat.

Chicken, Broccoli, and Millet Feast

Yield: 5 servings | Prep time: 15 minutes | Cook time: 30 minutes

Age: Adult dogs & Puppies (6 to 12 months)

Weight per serving: Suitable for Medium breeds (20-50 lbs)

Ingredients:

- 2 chicken thighs, boneless and skinless
- 1/2 cup millet
- 1/2 cup broccoli florets
- 2 cups chicken broth (low sodium)
- 1/4 cup pumpkin seeds

Directions:

1. Place chicken thighs and millet in a pot with chicken broth.
2. Simmer until chicken is cooked and millet is tender.
3. Add broccoli florets and simmer for an additional 5 minutes.
4. Once cooled, shred the chicken and stir in pumpkin seeds.

Nutritional Information (approx. per serving): 230 calories, 19g protein, 18g carbohydrates, 9g fat.

Ground Turkey & Sweet Pea Muffins

Yield: 6 muffins | Prep time: 15 minutes | Cook time: 20 minutes

Age: Adult dogs & Puppies (8 to 12 months)

Weight per muffin: Suitable for Small breeds (10-20 lbs)

Ingredients:

- 1/2 pound ground turkey
- 1 cup sweet peas, mashed
- 1 egg
- 1/2 cup oat flour
- 1/4 tsp baking powder

Directions:

1. Preheat oven to 375°F (190°C).
2. In a bowl, mix ground turkey, mashed peas, egg, oat flour, and baking powder.
3. Spoon mixture into a greased muffin tin.
4. Bake for 20 minutes or until set.
5. Allow muffins to cool completely before serving.

Nutritional Information (approx. per muffin): 120 calories, 10g protein, 8g carbohydrates, 4g fat.

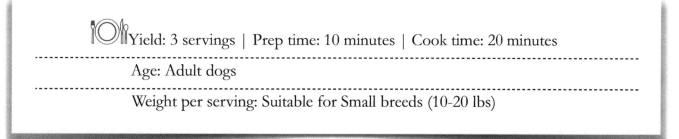

Chicken Heart & Rice Delight

Yield: 3 servings | Prep time: 10 minutes | Cook time: 20 minutes

Age: Adult dogs

Weight per serving: Suitable for Small breeds (10-20 lbs)

Ingredients:

- 1 pound chicken hearts
- 1 cup brown rice
- 2 cups chicken broth (low sodium)
- 1/4 cup broccoli florets
- 1 tbsp coconut oil

Directions:

1. In a pot, combine chicken hearts, rice, and chicken broth.
2. Bring to a boil, then reduce heat to simmer.
3. Add the broccoli florets and cook until rice is tender and hearts are cooked through.
4. Stir in coconut oil and let the dish cool before serving.

Nutritional Information (approx. per serving): 290 calories, 28g protein, 32g carbohydrates, 8g fat.

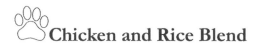 **Chicken and Rice Blend**

Yield: 3 servings | Prep time: 10 minutes | Cook time: 20 minutes

Age: Puppies (7 to 12 months) & Adult dogs

Weight per serving: Suitable for Medium breeds (30-60 lbs)

Ingredients:

- 1 pound boiled chicken breast, shredded
- 1 cup cooked white rice
- 1 tbsp olive oil
- 1/2 cup peas, steamed and mashed
- 1/4 cup carrot puree

Directions:

1. In a bowl, combine shredded chicken and cooked rice.
2. Mix in the mashed peas and carrot puree.
3. Drizzle with olive oil and mix thoroughly.
4. Let it cool before serving.

Nutritional Information (approx. per serving): 310 calories, 28g protein, 30g carbohydrates, 8g fat

Turkey and Barley Stew

🍽️ Yield: 3 servings | Prep time: 10 minutes | Cook time: 30 minutes

Age: Puppies (7 to 12 months) & Adult dogs

Weight per serving: Suitable for Medium breeds (30-60 lbs)

Ingredients:

- 1 pound turkey breast, diced
- 1 cup barley, cooked
- 1/2 cup green beans, chopped
- 1/4 cup carrots, diced
- 1/4 cup celery, diced • 1 tbsp olive oil

Directions:

1. In a pot, simmer turkey breast with enough water until fully cooked.
2. Add in the carrots, celery, and green beans, and let them cook until tender.
3. Stir in the cooked barley to the pot.
4. Add olive oil and mix well.
5. Let it cool before serving.

Nutritional Information (approx. per serving): 340 calories, 29g protein, 32g carbohydrates, 9g fat

Egg and Sweet Potato Scramble

🍽️ Yield: 2 servings | Prep time: 10 minutes | Cook time: 15 minutes

Age: Puppies (7 to 12 months) & Adult dogs

Weight per serving: Suitable for Medium breeds (30-60 lbs)

Ingredients:

- 3 large eggs
- 1 medium sweet potato
- 1 tbsp chia seeds
- 1 tbsp coconut oil or olive oil

Directions:

1. Start by peeling the sweet potato and cutting it into chunks.
2. Boil the sweet potato chunks until they are soft and can be easily mashed.
3. In a bowl, mash the sweet potato until smooth and set aside.
6. In a separate bowl, crack the eggs and whisk them until well-beaten.
7. Heat a skillet over medium heat and add coconut or olive oil.
8. Pour the beaten eggs into the skillet and scramble until nearly cooked through.
9. Mix in the mashed sweet potato and continue to cook until the eggs are fully done.
10. Remove from heat and let it cool.
11. Before serving, sprinkle chia seeds over the scramble.

Nutritional Information (approx. per serving): 290 calories, 14g protein, 28g carbohydrates, 14g fat

6.2 Fish-centric recipes

Herring & Broccoli Bliss

Yield: 4 servings | Prep time: 10 minutes | Cook time: 20 minutes

Age: Adult dogs & Puppies (8 to 14 months)

Weight per serving: Suitable for Medium breeds (25-55 lbs)

Ingredients:
- 1 pound herring, deboned and chopped
- 1 cup broccoli, finely chopped
- 1/2 cup peas
- 1 cup quinoa, cooked
- 1 tbsp fish oil

Directions:
1. Cook the herring in a skillet until it becomes flaky.
2. Add the broccoli and peas to the skillet and sauté until tender.
3. Mix in the cooked quinoa and fish oil, ensuring even distribution.
4. Let it cool before serving.

Nutritional Information (approx. per serving): 330 calories, 28g protein, 24g carbohydrates, 12g fat

Mackerel & Pumpkin Pie

Yield: 3 servings | Prep time: 15 minutes | Cook time: 25 minutes

Age: Adult dogs

Weight per serving: Suitable for Large breeds (50-90 lbs)

Ingredients:
- 1 pound mackerel, deboned and sliced
- 1 cup pumpkin puree
- 1/2 cup blueberries
- 1 cup barley, cooked
- 1 tbsp coconut oi

Directions:
1. In a skillet, cook the mackerel slices until they turn opaque.
2. In a mixing bowl, combine pumpkin puree, blueberries, and cooked barley.
3. Add the mackerel to the bowl and mix well, then drizzle with coconut oil.
4. Let it cool before serving.

Nutritional Information (approx. per serving): 370 calories, 30g protein, 28g carbohydrates, 16g fat

Sardine & Spinach Mix

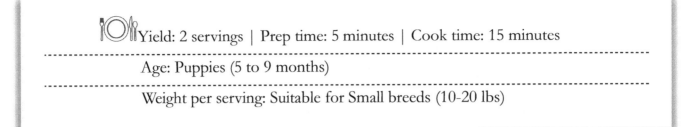

Yield: 2 servings | Prep time: 5 minutes | Cook time: 15 minutes

Age: Puppies (5 to 9 months)

Weight per serving: Suitable for Small breeds (10-20 lbs)

Ingredients:

- 1/2 pound sardines, deboned
- 1/2 cup spinach, finely chopped
- 1/4 cup carrots, diced
- 1/2 cup white rice, cooked
- 1 tsp flaxseed oil

Directions:

1. In a skillet, cook the sardines until they are heated through.
2. Add the spinach and carrots, cooking until the vegetables are tender.
3. Incorporate the cooked white rice into the mixture, then drizzle with flaxseed oil.
4. Let it cool before serving to your pup.

Nutritional Information (approx. per serving): 280 calories, 20g protein, 22g carbohydrates, 10g fat

Tilapia & Sweet Pea Treat

Yield: 4 servings | Prep time: 10 minutes | Cook time: 20 minutes

Age: Adult dogs & Puppies (9 to 15 months)

Weight per serving: Suitable for Medium breeds (20-50 lbs)

Ingredients:

- 1 pound tilapia fillets
- 1 cup sweet peas
- 1/2 cup carrots, shredded
- 1 cup couscous, cooked • 1 tbsp fish oil

Directions:

1. In a skillet, cook tilapia fillets until they flake easily with a fork.
2. Add sweet peas and shredded carrots to the skillet, cooking until tender.
3. Stir in the cooked couscous and fish oil, ensuring an even mix.
4. Once cooked, let the mixture cool before serving.

Nutritional Information (approx. per serving): 340 calories, 29g protein, 27g carbohydrates, 11g fat

Cod & Beet Medley

🍴 Yield: 3 servings | Prep time: 15 minutes | Cook time: 25 minutes

Age: Adult dogs

Weight per serving: Suitable for Large breeds (50-80 lbs)

Ingredients:
- 1 pound cod fillets
- 1/2 cup beets, diced
- 1/4 cup celery, chopped
- 1 cup millet, cooked
- 1 tsp olive oil

Directions:
1. Cook cod fillets in a skillet until they become flaky.
2. Add the diced beets and chopped celery, sautéing until tender.
3. Blend with the cooked millet in a mixing bowl and drizzle with olive oil.
4. Allow to cool before serving

Nutritional Information (approx. per serving): 360 calories, 31g protein, 30g carbohydrates, 13g fat

Trout & Apple Salad

🍴 Yield: 2 servings | Prep time: 10 minutes | Cook time: 15 minutes

Age: Puppies (6 to 12 months)

Weight per serving: Suitable for Small breeds (10-25 lbs)

Ingredients:
- 1/2 pound trout, deboned and sliced
- 1/2 apple, diced
- 1/4 cup spinach, finely chopped
- 1/2 cup barley, cooked
- 1 tsp chia seeds

Directions:
1. In a skillet, cook the trout slices until they turn opaque.
2. In a mixing bowl, combine apple dices, spinach, and cooked barley.
3. Add the trout to the bowl and sprinkle with chia seeds, mixing thoroughly.
4. Cool down before feeding.

Nutritional Information (approx. per serving): 290 calories, 21g protein, 25g carbohydrates, 9g fat

# Catfish & Veggie Stir-Fry

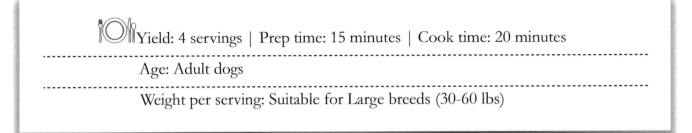

Yield: 4 servings | Prep time: 15 minutes | Cook time: 20 minutes

Age: Adult dogs

Weight per serving: Suitable for Large breeds (30-60 lbs)

Ingredients:

- 1 pound catfish, deboned and sliced
- 1/2 cup bell peppers, thinly sliced
- 1/2 cup snap peas
- 1 cup brown rice, cooked
- 1 tbsp coconut oil

Directions:

1. In a skillet, heat coconut oil and cook catfish slices until opaque.
2. Add bell peppers and snap peas, cooking until tender.
3. Blend with the cooked brown rice in a bowl, mixing thoroughly.
4. Allow to cool before serving.

Nutritional Information (approx. per serving): 310 calories, 28g protein, 29g carbohydrates, 9g fat

# Flounder & Berry Mix

Yield: 2 servings | Prep time: 10 minutes | Cook time: 15 minutes

Age: Puppies (8 to 14 months

Weight per serving: Suitable for Small breeds (10-25 lbs)

Ingredients:

- 1/2 pound flounder fillets
- 1/4 cup blueberries
- 1/4 cup cranberries
- 1/2 cup oatmeal, cooked
- 1 tsp flaxseed oil

Directions:

1. Cook flounder fillets in a pan until they flake easily.
2. In a bowl, combine blueberries, cranberries, and cooked oatmeal.
3. Mix in the flounder and drizzle with flaxseed oil.
4. Once mixed, let it cool before serving.

Nutritional Information (approx. per serving): 270 calories, 20g protein, 23g carbohydrates, 8g fat

🐾 Salmon & Green Bean Delight

🍽️ Yield: 4 servings | Prep time: 10 minutes | Cook time: 20 minutes

Age: Adult dogs & Senior dogs

Weight per serving: Suitable for Medium breeds (30-60 lbs)

Ingredients:

- 1 pound salmon fillet, deboned
- 1 cup green beans, chopped
- 1/2 cup zucchini, diced
- 1 cup bulgur wheat, cooked
- 1 tbsp fish oil

Directions:

5. Grill or pan-fry the salmon fillet until it flakes easily.
6. In a separate pan, sauté green beans and zucchini until tender.
7. In a mixing bowl, combine the salmon, vegetables, and bulgur wheat.
8. Drizzle with fish oil and mix well.
9. Allow to cool before serving.

Nutritional Information (approx. per serving): 350 calories, 30g protein, 28g carbohydrates, 12g fat

🐾 Tuna & Sweet Potato Mash

🍽️ Yield: 3 servings | Prep time: 15 minutes | Cook time: 20 minutes

Age: Adult dogs

Weight per serving: Suitable for Large breeds (50-80 lbs)

Ingredients:

- 1 pound tuna steaks
- 1 large sweet potato, cooked and mashed
- 1/4 cup peas
- 1/2 cup quinoa, cooked
- 1 tsp chia seeds

Directions:

1. Grill or pan-fry the tuna steaks until fully cooked.
2. In a large bowl, combine the tuna with mashed sweet potato.
3. Mix in peas, cooked quinoa, and chia seeds.
4. Ensure the mixture is cool before feeding.

Nutritional Information (approx. per serving): 370 calories, 33g protein, 32g carbohydrates, 10g fat

Whitefish & Cauliflower Rice

Yield: 2 servings | Prep time: 10 minutes | Cook time: 15 minutes

Age: Puppies (8 to 12 months)

Weight per serving: Suitable for Small breeds (15-30 lbs)

Ingredients:
- 1/2 pound whitefish, deboned
- 1 cup cauliflower, riced
- 1/4 cup broccoli florets
- 1/2 cup lentils, cooked
- 1 tsp olive oil

Directions:
1. Cook the whitefish in a skillet until it becomes opaque.
2. Add riced cauliflower and broccoli florets, cooking until tender.
3. Mix in the cooked lentils, and drizzle with olive oil.
4. Once cooled, it's ready to serve.

Nutritional Information (approx. per serving): 280 calories, 24g protein, 26g carbohydrates, 8g fat

Mackerel & Spinach Stew

Yield: 4 servings | Prep time: 15 minutes | Cook time: 25 minutes

Age: Adult dogs & Senior dog

Weight per serving: Suitable for Large breeds (60-90 lbs)

Ingredients:
- 1 pound mackerel, deboned and chopped
- 1 cup spinach, washed and roughly chopped
- 1/2 cup sweet potatoes, cubed
- 1 cup barley, cooked
- 2 tbsp fish broth

Directions:
1. In a pot, combine mackerel pieces and fish broth, then bring to a gentle simmer.
2. Once the mackerel starts to cook, add in sweet potatoes.
3. When the potatoes are nearly done, add spinach and cook until wilted.
4. Finally, stir in the cooked barley, mixing well.
5. Remove from heat and let it cool before serving.

Nutritional Information (approx. per serving): 380 calories, 31g protein, 30g carbohydrates, 12g fat

Sardine & Carrot Pasta

Yield: 2 servings | Prep time: 10 minutes | Cook time: 20 minutes

Age: Puppies (7 to 13 months)

Weight per serving: Suitable for Medium breeds (25-45 lbs)

Ingredients:

- 1 cup sardines, deboned
- 1/2 cup carrots, julienned
- 1/4 cup green peas
- 1 cup whole wheat pasta, cooked
- 1 tsp flaxseed oil

Directions:

1. In a skillet, heat sardines on low until they're warmed through.
2. Add julienned carrots and green peas, cooking until the carrots are tender.
3. Mix in the cooked whole wheat pasta.
4. Drizzle with flaxseed oil, then stir well.
5. After cooling, serve to your furry friend.

Nutritional Information (approx. per serving): 320 calories, 28g protein, 29g carbohydrates, 10g fat

Haddock & Butternut Bowl

Yield: 4 servings | Prep time: 15 minutes | Cook time: 25 minutes

Age: Adult dogs

Weight per serving: Suitable for Medium breeds (30-60 lbs)

Ingredients:

- 1 pound haddock, deboned and sliced
- 1 cup butternut squash, cubed
- 1/2 cup green beans, chopped
- 1 cup wild rice, cooked
- 1 tbsp olive oil

Directions:

1. In a skillet, cook haddock slices until opaque.
2. Add butternut squash cubes and cook until slightly tender.
3. Stir in the green beans and cook until they're bright green and tender.
4. Combine everything with the wild rice in a bowl and drizzle with olive oil.
5. Allow to cool before serving.

Nutritional Information (approx. per serving): 330 calories, 29g protein, 31g carbohydrates, 9g fat

Prawn & Lentil Feast

Yield: 3 servings | Prep time: 10 minutes | Cook time: 20 minutes

Age: Senior dogs

Weight per serving: Suitable for Small breeds (10-25 lbs)

Ingredients:

- 1 cup prawns, deveined and shelled
- 1/2 cup lentils, cooked
- 1/4 cup bell peppers, diced
- 1/2 cup quinoa, cooked
- 1 tsp coconut oil

Directions:

1. In a skillet, sauté prawns with coconut oil until they turn pink.
2. Add bell peppers, cooking until they're tender.
3. Combine prawns and peppers with lentils and quinoa in a bowl, mixing well.
4. Let the mixture cool before serving.

Nutritional Information (approx. per serving): 270 calories, 23g protein, 25g carbohydrates, 6g fat

Sole & Asparagus Blend

Yield: 2 servings | Prep time: 10 minutes | Cook time: 15 minutes

Age: Puppies (8 to 14 months)

Weight per serving: Suitable for Medium breeds (20-50 lbs

Ingredients:

- 1/2 pound sole, deboned
- 1/2 cup asparagus, sliced
- 1/4 cup cherry tomatoes, halved
- 1 cup millet, cooked
- 1 tsp fish oil

Directions:

1. Pan-fry the sole until it flakes easily.
2. In another pan, sauté asparagus slices and cherry tomatoes until the asparagus is tender.
3. Blend sole, asparagus, tomatoes, and millet in a bowl.
4. Drizzle with fish oil and mix.
5. Once cooled, serve to your canine companion.

Nutritional Information (approx. per serving): 290 calories, 26g protein, 28g carbohydrates, 8g fat

Cod & Pumpkin Puree

Yield: 3 servings | Prep time: 10 minutes | Cook time: 20 minutes

Age: Puppies (7 to 12 months) & Adult dogs

Weight per serving: Suitable for Medium breeds (30-60 lbs)

Ingredients:
- 1 pound cod, deboned
- 1 cup pumpkin puree
- 1/2 cup broccoli florets, finely chopped
- 1/2 cup brown rice, cooked
- 1 tbsp salmon oil

Directions:
1. Steam or grill the cod until it flakes easily.
2. In a bowl, mix the cooked cod with pumpkin puree.
3. Stir in finely chopped broccoli florets.
4. Blend in the cooked brown rice.
5. Drizzle with salmon oil and mix thoroughly.
6. Let it cool before serving.

Nutritional Information (approx. per serving): 340 calories, 30g protein, 28g carbohydrates, 11g fat

Tilapia & Beet Salad

Yield: 4 servings | Prep time: 15 minutes | Cook time: 20 minutes

Age: Adult dogs

Weight per serving: Suitable for Large breeds (50-80 lbs)

Ingredients:
- 1 pound tilapia, deboned
- 1/2 cup beets, diced and steamed
- 1/4 cup carrots, grated
- 1/2 cup couscous, cooked
- 1 tsp flaxseed oil

Directions:
1. Cook the tilapia in a skillet or oven until fully done.
2. In a large bowl, combine the tilapia, steamed beets, and grated carrots.
3. Mix in the cooked couscous.
4. Finish with a drizzle of flaxseed oil, mixing well.
5. Once cooled, it's ready to be served

Nutritional Information (approx. per serving): 360 calories, 32g protein, 29g carbohydrates, 10g fat

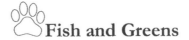
Fish and Greens

Yield: 3 servings | Prep time: 10 minutes | Cook time: 20 minutes

Age: Puppies (7 to 12 months) & Adult dogs

Weight per serving: Suitable for Medium breeds (30-60 lbs

Ingredients:

- 1 pound mackerel, deboned
- 1 cup spinach, steamed and chopped
- 1/2 cup zucchini, finely sliced
- 1 tbsp fish oil
- 1/4 cup quinoa, cooked

Directions:

1. Steam or grill the mackerel until it flakes easily.
2. In a bowl, flake the cooked mackerel and add chopped spinach.
3. Integrate finely sliced zucchini.
4. Blend in the cooked quinoa.
5. Drizzle with fish oil and mix well.
6. Let it cool before serving.

Nutritional Information (approx. per serving): 320 calories, 31g protein, 22g carbohydrates, 12g fat

Salmon and Lentil Delight

Yield: 3 servings | Prep time: 15 minutes | Cook time: 25 minutes

Age: Puppies (7 to 12 months) & Adult dogs

Weight per serving: Suitable for Medium breeds (30-60 lbs)

Ingredients:

- 1 pound salmon fillet
- 1/2 cup lentils, cooked
- 1/4 cup spinach, finely chopped
- 1/2 cup carrot, shredded
- 1 tbsp fish oil

Directions:

1. Steam or grill the salmon fillet until it's cooked through.
2. In a bowl, flake the salmon into smaller chunks.
3. Add cooked lentils, finely chopped spinach, and shredded carrot.
4. Drizzle fish oil and mix well.
5. Let the mixture cool before serving.

Nutritional Information (approx. per serving): 350 calories, 31g protein, 25g carbohydrates, 15g fat

6.3 Red meat dishes

Beef & Vegetable Medley

🍽️ Yield: 4 servings | Prep time: 15 minutes | Cook time: 25 minutes

----

Age: Adult dogs & Puppies (7 to 12 months

Weight per serving: Suitable for Medium breeds (20-50 lbs

Ingredients:
- 1 pound lean ground beef
- 1/2 cup carrots, diced
- 1/2 cup green beans, chopped
- 1 cup brown rice, cooked
- 1 tbsp olive oil

Directions:
1. Cook the ground beef in a skillet until browned.
2. Add the carrots and green beans to the skillet and cook until tender.
3. Mix in the cooked brown rice and olive oil, stirring thoroughly.
4. Let it cool before serving.

Nutritional Information (approx. per serving): 320 calories, 22g protein, 26g carbohydrates, 14g fat.

Pork & Pea Casserole

🍽️ Yield: 4 servings | Prep time: 15 minutes | Cook time: 35 minutes

----

Age: Adult dogs & Puppies (8 to 12 months)

Weight per serving: Suitable for Large breeds (50-100 lbs)

Ingredients:
- 1 pound pork loin, diced
- 1 cup peas
- 1/2 cup rolled oats
- 1 cup chicken broth (low sodium)
- 1 tbsp olive oil

Directions:
1. Preheat oven to 375°F (190°C).
2. In a pan, cook the diced pork loin until browned.
3. Mix pork, peas, rolled oats, and olive oil in a casserole dish.
4. Pour in chicken broth.
5. Bake in the oven for 20 minutes. Allow to cool before serving.

Nutritional Information (approx. per serving): 350 calories, 28g protein, 22g carbohydrates, 15g fat.

Beef & Blueberry Muffins

Yield: 6 muffins | Prep time: 20 minutes | Cook time: 25 minutes

Age: Adult dogs

Weight per muffin: Suitable for Small breeds (10-20 lbs)

Ingredients:
- 1/2 pound lean ground beef
- 1/2 cup blueberries
- 1 egg
- 1 cup oat flour
- 1/4 tsp baking soda

Directions:
1. Preheat oven to 375°F (190°C).
2. Mix ground beef, blueberries, egg, oat flour, and baking soda in a bowl.
3. Spoon the mixture into muffin tins.
4. Bake in the oven for 20–25 minutes or until done.
5. Allow to cool before serving.

Nutritional Information (approx. per muffin): 220 calories, 15g protein, 18g carbohydrates, 9g fat.

Lamb & Lentil Mix

Yield: 4 servings | Prep time: 15 minutes | Cook time: 30 minutes

Age: Adult dogs & Puppies (9 to 12 months) s

Weight per serving: Suitable for Large breeds (50-100 lbs)

Ingredients:
- 1 pound lamb meat, diced
- 1 cup lentils, cooked
- 1/2 cup carrots, diced
- 2 cups beef broth (low sodium)
- 1 tbsp flaxseed oil

Directions:
1. In a pot, brown the diced lamb meat.
2. Add carrots and cooked lentils.
3. Pour in beef broth and simmer for 20 minutes or until lamb is tender.
4. Remove from heat, stir in flaxseed oil, and let cool before serving

Nutritional Information (approx. per serving): 370 calories, 30g protein, 24g carbohydrates, 16g fat.

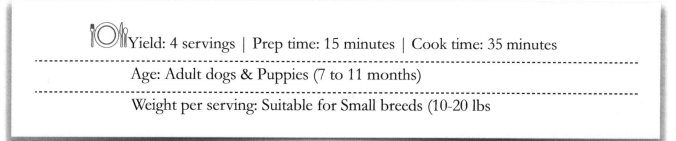

Beef Liver & Sweet Potato Mash

Yield: 4 servings | Prep time: 15 minutes | Cook time: 35 minutes

Age: Adult dogs & Puppies (7 to 11 months)

Weight per serving: Suitable for Small breeds (10-20 lbs

Ingredients:

- 1/2 pound beef liver, finely chopped
- 1 cup sweet potato, mashed
- 1/2 cup peas
- 1 tbsp olive oil
- Pinch of parsley, dried

Directions:

1. In a pan, sauté the beef liver until fully cooked.
2. Mix in mashed sweet potato, peas, olive oil, and dried parsley.
3. Cook on low heat for an additional 10 minutes, stirring occasionally.
4. Let the mixture cool before serving to your dog.

Nutritional Information (approx. per serving): 280 calories, 22g protein, 20g carbohydrates, 10g fat.

 **Classic Beef & Rice**

Yield: 3 servings | Prep time: 10 minutes | Cook time: 20 minutes

Age: Adult dogs & Puppies (9 to 12 months)

Weight per serving: Suitable for Large breeds (50-100 lbs)

Ingredients:

- 1/2 pound beef chunks
- 1 cup rice, cooked
- 1/2 cup green beans, chopped
- 1/4 cup carrots, finely diced
- 1 tbsp coconut oil

Directions:

1. Cook beef chunks in a pan until browned.
2. Add green beans and carrots, cooking until tender.
3. Mix in the cooked rice and combine well.
4. Turn off heat and stir in coconut oil for added moisture and nutrition.
5. Once cooled, it's ready to be served.

Nutritional Information (approx. per serving): 320 calories, 25g protein, 35g carbohydrates, 10g fat.

Pork & Pumpkin Medley

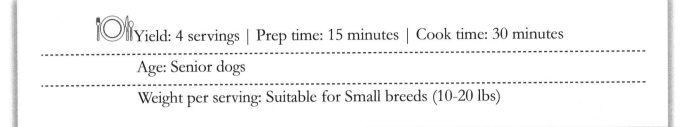

Yield: 4 servings | Prep time: 15 minutes | Cook time: 30 minutes

---
Age: Senior dogs

Weight per serving: Suitable for Small breeds (10-20 lbs)

Ingredients:

- 1/2 pound pork loin, diced
- 1 cup pumpkin puree
- 1/2 cup zucchini, sliced
- 1 tbsp fish oil
- Pinch of turmeric

Directions:

1. In a skillet, cook the pork pieces until fully cooked.
2. Add in zucchini slices, cooking for another 10 minutes.
3. Stir in pumpkin puree, fish oil, and a pinch of turmeric.
4. Cook on low heat until all ingredients are well-combined and heated.
5. Cool before serving to your canine friend.

Nutritional Information (approx. per serving): 270 calories, 20g protein, 15g carbohydrates, 12g fat.

Meaty Mutton & Potato Mash

Yield: 3 servings | Prep time: 15 minutes | Cook time: 35 minutes

---
Age: Adult dogs

Weight per serving: Suitable for Medium breeds (20-50 lbs)

Ingredients:

- 1 pound mutton, diced
- 1 cup potatoes, mashed
- 1/2 cup peas
- 2 cups beef broth (low sodium)
- 1 tbsp flaxseed oil

Directions:

1. In a pot, cook the mutton pieces until browned.
2. Add the beef broth and simmer for 20 minutes.
3. Add peas and continue cooking for another 10 minutes.
4. Mix in the mashed potatoes until well combined.
5. Before serving, stir in the flaxseed oil.

Nutritional Information (approx. per serving): 390 calories, 30g protein, 32g carbohydrates, 16g fat.

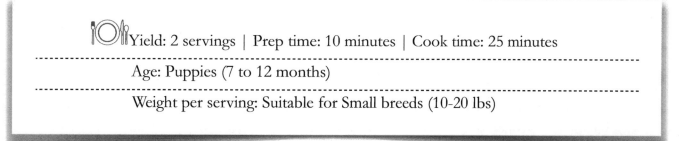

Beef & Blueberry Fusion

Yield: 2 servings | Prep time: 10 minutes | Cook time: 25 minutes

Age: Puppies (7 to 12 months)

Weight per serving: Suitable for Small breeds (10-20 lbs)

Ingredients:

- 1/2 pound ground beef
- 1/2 cup blueberries
- 1/4 cup carrots, shredded
- 1 cup brown rice, cooked
- 1 tbsp olive oil

Directions:

1. In a skillet, brown the ground beef.
2. Add shredded carrots and cook for another 5 minutes.
3. Mix in the cooked brown rice and blueberries.
4. Simmer for 10 minutes.
5. Drizzle olive oil over the top before serving.

Nutritional Information (approx. per serving): 310 calories, 24g protein, 40g carbohydrates, 8g fat.

Pork & Apple Delight

Yield: 4 servings | Prep time: 10 minutes | Cook time: 30 minutes

Age: Senior dogs

Weight per serving: Suitable for Medium breeds (20-50 lbs)

Ingredients:

- 1 pound pork meat, diced
- 1 apple, cored and diced
- 1/2 cup green beans, chopped
- 1 cup quinoa, cooked
- 1 tbsp fish oil

Directions:

1. Cook the pork in a pot until browned.
2. Add chopped green beans and diced apple, cooking until tender.
3. Mix in the cooked quinoa, stirring well.
4. Add fish oil and mix again.
5. Serve once cooled.

Nutritional Information (approx. per serving): 330 calories, 28g protein, 35g carbohydrates, 9g fat.

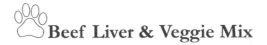

Beef Liver & Veggie Mix

Yield: 3 servings | Prep time: 15 minutes | Cook time: 20 minutes

Age: Adult dogs & Puppies (9 to 12 months)

Weight per serving: Suitable for Large breeds (50-100 lbs

Ingredients:

- 1/2 pound beef liver, sliced
- 1/2 cup broccoli, steamed and chopped
- 1/2 cup cauliflower, steamed and mashed
- 2 tbsp coconut oil
- Pinch of rosemary

Directions:

1. In a skillet, cook beef liver slices until well-done.
2. Mix in steamed broccoli and mashed cauliflower.
3. Add coconut oil and a pinch of rosemary for flavor.
4. Stir until all ingredients are well-mixed and heated.
5. Cool down before serving.

Nutritional Information (approx. per serving): 320 calories, 29g protein, 18g carbohydrates, 15g fat.

Lamb & Pumpkin Stew

Yield: 4 servings | Prep time: 15 minutes | Cook time: 40 minutes

Age: Adult dogs & Puppies (6 to 12 months)

Weight per serving: Suitable for Medium breeds (20-50 lbs

Ingredients:

- 1 pound lamb meat, diced
- 1 cup pumpkin puree
- 1/2 cup zucchini, sliced
- 2 cups lamb or beef broth (low sodium)
- 1 tbsp chia seeds

Directions:

1. In a pot, brown the lamb meat.
2. Add the lamb or beef broth and bring to a boil.
3. Stir in the pumpkin puree and sliced zucchini.
4. Simmer for 30 minutes or until the lamb is tender.
5. Mix in the chia seeds and let it cool before serving.

Nutritional Information (approx. per serving): 350 calories, 31g protein, 24g carbohydrates, 14g fat.

Beef & Green Bean Casserole

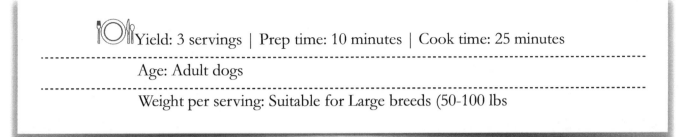

Yield: 3 servings | Prep time: 10 minutes | Cook time: 25 minutes

Age: Adult dogs

Weight per serving: Suitable for Large breeds (50-100 lbs

Ingredients:

- 1 pound ground beef
- 1 cup green beans, chopped
- 1/2 cup carrots, grated
- 1/2 cup peas
- 1 tbsp olive oil

Directions:

1. Preheat oven to 375°F (190°C).
2. In a skillet, brown the ground beef and drain off any excess fat.
3. Mix the beef with chopped green beans, grated carrots, and peas in a baking dish.
4. Drizzle with olive oil.
5. Bake for 20 minutes or until the top becomes lightly browned.
6. Let it cool before serving.

Nutritional Information (approx. per serving): 360 calories, 32g protein, 18g carbohydrates, 16g fat.

Beef Heart & Vegetable Stir-fry

Yield: 3 servings | Prep time: 10 minutes | Cook time: 20 minutes

Age: Adult dogs

Weight per serving: Suitable for Large breeds (50-100 lbs)

Ingredients:

- 1 pound beef heart, thinly sliced
- 1/2 cup bell peppers, sliced
- 1/4 cup zucchini, diced
- 2 tbsp olive oil
- A pinch of turmeric

Directions:

1. In a pan, heat olive oil and stir-fry beef heart slices until browned.
2. Add bell peppers and zucchini, continuing to stir-fry until vegetables are tender.
3. Sprinkle with turmeric and stir well.
4. Allow to cool before serving.

Nutritional Information (approx. per serving): 285 calories, 31g protein, 10g carbohydrates, 14g fat.

Ground Beef & Broccoli Pie

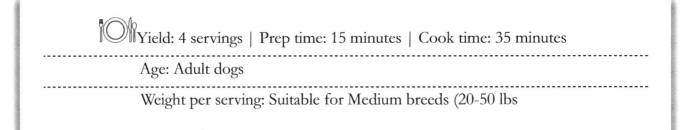

Yield: 4 servings | Prep time: 15 minutes | Cook time: 35 minutes

Age: Adult dogs

Weight per serving: Suitable for Medium breeds (20-50 lbs

Ingredients:

- 1 pound ground beef
- 1 cup broccoli florets, steamed and mashed
- 1/2 cup rolled oats
- 1 egg
- 2 tbsp flaxseed oil

Directions:

1. Preheat the oven to 350°F (175°C).
2. In a mixing bowl, combine ground beef, mashed broccoli, rolled oats, and egg.
3. Spread the mixture into a pie dish and bake for 30 minutes or until the beef is cooked through.
4. Drizzle flaxseed oil over the top once cooled.

Nutritional Information (approx. per serving): 310 calories, 25g protein, 15g carbohydrates, 18g fat

Pork and Vegetable Blend

Yield: 3 servings | Prep time: 15 minutes | Cook time: 25 minutes

Age: Puppies (7 to 12 months) & Adult dogs

Weight per serving: Suitable for Medium breeds (30-60 lbs)

Ingredients:

- 1 pound lean pork, diced
- 1/2 cup bell peppers, finely chopped
- 1/2 cup broccoli florets
- 1/4 cup peas
- 1 tbsp coconut oil

Directions:

1. In a pan, sauté the diced pork in coconut oil until fully cooked.
2. Add the bell peppers, broccoli, and peas, and stir-fry until they are soft but still have a crunch.
3. Transfer to a bowl and allow to cool.
4. Serve in portions suitable for your dog's size and appetite.

Nutritional Information (approx. per serving): 360 calories, 30g protein, 15g carbohydrates, 18g fat

 **Lamb and Carrot Stew**

Yield: 3 servings | Prep time: 10 minutes | Cook time: 40 minutes

Age: Puppies (7 to 12 months) & Adult dogs

Weight per serving: Suitable for Medium breeds (30-60 lbs)

Ingredients:
- 1 pound lamb chunks
- 1 cup carrots, diced
- 1/2 cup green beans, chopped
- 1 tbsp olive oil
- 1/2 cup barley, cooked

Directions:
1. In a pot, add lamb chunks with enough water and bring to a simmer.
2. Cook until the lamb is tender.
3. Add diced carrots and green beans to the pot and cook until they are tender.
4. Stir in the cooked barley.
5. Drizzle with olive oil and mix well.
6. Allow the stew to cool before serving.

Nutritional Information (approx. per serving): 380 calories, 32g protein, 27g carbohydrates, 16g fat

 **Beef and Quinoa Mix**

Yield: 3 servings | Prep time: 10 minutes | Cook time: 20 minutes

Age: Puppies (7 to 12 months) & Adult dogs

Weight per serving: Suitable for Medium breeds (30-60 lbs)

Ingredients:
- 1 pound ground beef (lean)
- 1 cup cooked quinoa
- 1/2 cup zucchini, finely chopped
- 1/2 cup red bell pepper, finely chopped
- 1 tbsp flaxseed oil

Directions:
1. Cook the ground beef in a pan until fully browned.
2. In a bowl, combine the cooked beef and quinoa.
3. Stir in finely chopped zucchini and red bell pepper.
4. Drizzle with flaxseed oil and mix thoroughly.
5. Let it cool before serving.

Nutritional Information (approx. per serving): 365 calories, 33g protein, 20g carbohydrates, 15g fat

6.4 Vegetarian options

 Chickpea & Spinach Stew

Yield: 4 servings | Prep time: 10 minutes | Cook time: 20 minutes

Age: Suitable for dogs aged 8 months and above

Weight per Serving: For dogs weighing 25-35 lbs

Ingredients:

- 2 cups chickpeas, cooked
- 1 cup spinach, chopped
- 1 carrot, diced
- 1 tbsp olive oil
- 2 cups water

Directions:

1. Heat olive oil in a pot on medium heat.
2. Sauté diced carrot for 3 minutes.
3. Add chickpeas and water, bring to a boil.
4. Simmer for 10 minutes.
5. Mix in spinach, cook until wilted.

Nutritional Info (approx. per serving): 250 calories, 10g protein, 38g carbohydrates, 5g fat

 Rice & Veggies Medley

Yield: 6 servings | Prep time: 10 minutes | Cook time: 20 minutes

Age: Suitable for dogs aged 7 months and above

Weight per Serving: For dogs weighing 20-28 lbs

Ingredients:

- 1 cup rice
- 1/2 cup peas
- 1 carrot, diced
- 2 cups water
- 1 tbsp flaxseed oil

Directions:

1. In a pot, bring the 2 cups of water to boil.
2. Add rice and diced carrot, reduce heat to a simmer.
3. Cook for 15 minutes or until rice is almost done.
4. Stir in peas and cook for an additional 5 minutes.
5. Remove from heat and stir in flaxseed oil.

Nutritional Info (approx. per serving): 215 calories, 6g protein, 34g carbohydrates, 5g fat

Sweet Potato & Tofu Delight

Yield: 4 servings | Prep time: 15 minutes | Cook time: 25 minutes

Age: Suitable for dogs aged 7 months and above

Weight per Serving: For dogs weighing 28-38 lbs

Ingredients:
- 2 large sweet potatoes, peeled and cubed
- 1 cup tofu, cubed
- 1 tbsp olive oil
- 1/4 cup peas
- 2 tbsp flaxseed, ground

Directions:
1. Preheat the oven to 375°F.
2. Toss sweet potato cubes and tofu with olive oil in a bowl.
3. Spread the mixture on a baking sheet in a single layer.
4. Roast in the oven for 20 minutes, or until sweet potatoes are tender.
5. Remove from oven, stir in peas, and roast for an additional 5 minutes.
6. Once done, sprinkle ground flaxseed over the mix.

Nutritional Info (approx. per serving): 265 calories, 11g protein, 35g carbohydrates, 8g fat

Quinoa & Veggie Bowl

Yield: 6 servings | Prep time: 10 minutes | Cook time: 20 minutes

Age: Suitable for dogs aged 9 months and above

Weight per Serving: For dogs weighing 24-32 lbs

Ingredients:
- 1 cup quinoa
- 2 cups water
- 1 carrot, diced
- 1/2 cup green beans, chopped
- 1 tbsp coconut oil

Directions:
1. Rinse quinoa under cold water until water runs clear.
2. In a pot, bring the 2 cups of water to a boil.
3. Add quinoa and reduce heat to low, covering the pot.
4. After 10 minutes, add diced carrot and chopped green beans.
5. Continue cooking for another 10 minutes
6. Remove from heat and stir in coconut oil

Nutritional Info (approx. per serving): 220 calories, 8g protein, 35g carbohydrates, 5g fat

Rice & Lentil Fusion

Yield: 4 servings | Prep time: 10 minutes | Cook time: 30 minutes

Age: Suitable for dogs aged 8 months and above

Weight per Serving: For dogs weighing 28-40 lbs

Ingredients:

- 1 cup brown rice
- 1/2 cup lentils
- 2.5 cups water
- 1/2 bell pepper, diced
- 1 tbsp olive oil

Directions:

1. Rinse brown rice and lentils separately under cold water.
2. In a pot, combine the water, brown rice, and lentils. Bring to a boil.
3. Reduce heat to a simmer and cover. Cook for 20 minutes.
4. Stir in diced bell pepper and continue to cook for another 10 minutes
5. Remove from heat, drizzle with olive oil, and stir until well combined.

Nutritional Info (approx. per serving): 240 calories, 10g protein, 40g carbohydrates, 4g fat

Cauliflower & Chia Seed Mix

Yield: 5 servings | Prep time: 15 minutes | Cook time: 25 minutes

Age: Suitable for dogs aged 7 months and above

Weight per Serving: For dogs weighing 20-30 lbs

Ingredients:

- 1 cauliflower head, chopped
- 2 tbsp chia seeds, soaked
- 1 tbsp coconut oil
- 1/4 cup chopped parsley
- 2 cups cooked barley

Directions:

1. Steam cauliflower until tender.
2. In a bowl, mix steamed cauliflower, chia seeds, and barley.
3. Stir in coconut oil and parsley.
4. Let cool before serving.

Nutritional Info (approx. per serving): 210 calories, 7g protein, 30g carbohydrates, 6g fat

Carrot & Bean Casserole

Yield: 4 servings | Prep time: 10 minutes | Cook time: 20 minutes

Age: Suitable for dogs aged 8 months and above

Weight per Serving: For dogs weighing 25-35 lbs

Ingredients:

- 3 large carrots, diced
- 1 cup green beans, chopped
- 2 cups cooked bulgur wheat
- 1 tbsp olive oil
-

Directions:

1. Steam carrots and green beans until tender.
2. In a bowl, combine veggies with bulgur wheat.
3. Mix in olive oil.
4. Let cool before serving.

Nutritional Info (approx. per serving): 220 calories, 6g protein, 40g carbohydrates, 4g fat

Pumpkin & Tempeh Treat

Yield: 5 servings | Prep time: 10 minutes | Cook time: 25 minutes

Age: Suitable for dogs aged 9 months and above

Weight per Serving: For dogs weighing 20-28 lbs

Ingredients:

- 1 cup pumpkin puree
- 1 cup tempeh, crumbled
- 1/2 cup cooked quinoa
- 1 tbsp flaxseed oil

Directions:

1. In a pan, lightly fry tempeh until golden.
2. Mix tempeh, pumpkin puree, and quinoa in a bowl.
3. Stir in flaxseed oil.
4. Let cool before serving

Nutritional Info (approx. per serving): 240 calories, 11g protein, 30g carbohydrates, 8g fat

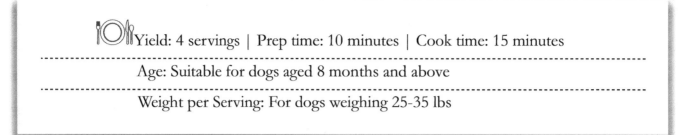 Broccoli & Cottage Cheese Platter

Yield: 4 servings | Prep time: 10 minutes | Cook time: 15 minutes

Age: Suitable for dogs aged 8 months and above

Weight per Serving: For dogs weighing 25-35 lbs

Ingredients:
- 2 cups broccoli florets
- 1 cup cottage cheese
- 1 cup cooked millet
- 1 tbsp olive oil

Directions:
1. Steam the broccoli florets until tender.
2. In a bowl, combine broccoli, cottage cheese, and millet.
3. Drizzle with olive oil and mix well.
4. Let cool before serving.

Nutritional Info (approx. per serving): 230 calories, 12g protein, 28g carbohydrates, 7g fat

 Beet & Brown Rice Bowl

Yield: 5 servings | Prep time: 15 minutes | Cook time: 35 minutes

Age: Suitable for dogs aged 9 months and above

Weight per Serving: For dogs weighing 20-30 lbs

Ingredients:
- 2 medium beets, peeled and diced
- 2 cups cooked brown rice
- 1/2 cup peas
- 1 tbsp flaxseed oil

Directions:
1. Steam the diced beets until soft.
2. In a bowl, mix beets, brown rice, and peas.
3. Drizzle with flaxseed oil and combine well.
4. Let cool before serving.

Nutritional Info (approx. per serving): 210 calories, 6g protein, 38g carbohydrates, 4g fat

Parsnip & Lentil Medley

Yield: 6 servings | Prep time: 10 minutes | Cook time: 30 minutes

Age: Suitable for dogs aged 10 months and above

Weight per Serving: For dogs weighing 25-37 lbs

Ingredients:

- 2 large parsnips, diced
- 1 cup green lentils
- 3 cups water
- 1 tbsp coconut oil

Directions:

1. In a pot, cook lentils and parsnips with water until lentils are tender.
2. Drain any excess water.
3. Mix in coconut oil while still warm.
4. Let cool before serving.

Nutritional Info (approx. per serving): 220 calories, 9g protein, 40g carbohydrates, 3g fat

Potato & Green Bean Blend

Yield: 4 servings | Prep time: 10 minutes | Cook time: 25 minutes

Age: Suitable for dogs aged 9 months and above

Weight per Serving: For dogs weighing 30-40 lbs

Ingredients:

- 3 medium potatoes, peeled and diced
- 1 cup green beans, chopped
- 1 tbsp olive oil
- 2 tbsp nutritional yeast

Directions:

1. Boil the potatoes until tender. Drain and mash them.
2. Steam the green beans until soft.
3. In a bowl, mix mashed potatoes, green beans, olive oil, and nutritional yeast.
4. Let cool before serving.

Nutritional Info (approx. per serving): 235 calories, 8g protein, 40g carbohydrates, 5g fat

Oats & Vegetable Pottage

Yield: 5 servings | Prep time: 10 minutes | Cook time: 20 minutes

Age: Suitable for dogs aged 7 months and above

Weight per Serving: For dogs weighing 20-28 lbs

Ingredients:
- 2 cups rolled oats
- 1 carrot, diced
- 1/2 cup peas
- 1/4 cup sunflower seeds
- 4 cups water

Directions:
1. In a pot, cook oats, carrot, and peas in water until oats are soft.
2. Remove from heat and stir in sunflower seeds.
3. Let cool before serving.

Nutritional Info (approx. per serving): 210 calories, 7g protein, 32g carbohydrates, 6g fat

Buckwheat & Red Bell Pepper Chow

Yield: 4 servings | Prep time: 15 minutes | Cook time: 25 minutes

Age: Suitable for dogs aged 10 months and above

Weight per Serving: For dogs weighing 30-40 lbs

Ingredients:
- 1 cup buckwheat
- 2 red bell peppers, diced
- 1 tbsp coconut oil
- 2.5 cups water
- 1/4 cup parsley, chopped

Directions:
1. Cook buckwheat in water until soft.
2. Sauté bell peppers in coconut oil until tender.
3. Mix buckwheat, bell peppers, and parsley in a bowl.
4. Let cool before serving.

Nutritional Info (approx. per serving): 230 calories, 8g protein, 38g carbohydrates, 5g fat

Chapter 7: Healthy Treats and Snacks

7.1 Biscuits and cookies

Peanut Butter Banana Bites

Yield: 4 servings | Prep time: 10 minutes | Cook time: 15 minutes

Age: 6+ months

Weight per Serving: 20g

Ingredients:
- 1 ripe banana, mashed
- 1/2 cup oat flour
- 2 tbsp peanut butter (ensure no xylitol)

Directions:
1. Preheat oven to 350°F.
2. Mix all ingredients in a bowl.
3. Roll into small balls and place on a baking sheet.
4. Bake for 15 minutes or until golden brown.

Nutritional Information: 90 calories, 3g protein, 12g carbohydrates, 4g fat

Pumpkin Carrot Sticks

Yield: 6 servings | Prep time: 15 minutes | Cook time: 25 minutes

Age: 4+ months

Weight per Serving: 25g

Ingredients:
- 1/2 cup pumpkin puree
- 1 carrot, grated
- 1 cup whole wheat flour

Directions:
1. Preheat oven to 350°F.
2. Mix ingredients and knead into a dough.
3. Roll out and cut into stick shapes.
4. Bake until crispy.

Nutritional Information: 70 calories, 2g protein, 14g carbohydrates, 0.5g fat

Coconut Apple Rings

🍽 Yield: 2 servings | Prep time: 10 minutes | Cook time: 0 minutes

Age: 5+ months

Weight per Serving: 50g

Ingredients:
- 1 apple, cored and sliced into rings
- 2 tbsp melted coconut oil

Directions:
1. Dip apple rings in coconut oil.
2. Place on a tray and freeze until set.

Nutritional Information: 110 calories, 0.5g protein, 20g carbohydrates, 6g fat

Sweet Potato Chews

🍽 Yield: 4 servings | Prep time: 10 minutes | Cook time: 2-3 hours

Age: 6+ months

Weight per Serving: 30g

Ingredients:
- 1 large sweet potato, sliced

Directions:
1. Preheat oven to 250°F.
2. Lay slices on a baking sheet.
3. Bake for 2-3 hours, turning occasionally until dried.

Nutritional Information: 70 calories, 1g protein, 17g carbohydrates, 0.1g fat

 **Chicken & Parsley Biscuits**

Yield: 4 servings | Prep time: 15 minutes | Cook time: 20 minutes

Age: 8+ months

Weight per Serving: 20g

Ingredients:
- 1 cup cooked chicken, finely chopped
- 1 tbsp fresh parsley, chopped
- 1 cup oat flour

Directions:
1. Preheat oven to 350°F.
2. Mix ingredients and roll into balls.
3. Flatten and bake until golden.

Nutritional Information: 110 calories, 8g protein, 12g carbohydrates, 3g fat

 **Berry Bone Biscuits**

Yield: 6 servings | Prep time: 10 minutes | Cook time: 18 minutes

Age: 6+ months

Weight per Serving: 25g

Ingredients:
- 1/2 cup mixed berries, mashed
- 1.5 cups whole wheat flour

Directions:
1. Preheat oven to 350°F.
2. Mix ingredients and roll out.
3. Cut into bone shapes and bake.

Nutritional Information: 85 calories, 3g protein, 17g carbohydrates, 0.5g fat

🐾 Oat & Honey Cookies

🍽 Yield: 4 servings | Prep time: 10 minutes | Cook time: 15 minutes

Age: 8+ months

Weight per Serving: 20g

Ingredients:
- 1 cup oats
- 1 tbsp honey
- 1/4 cup water

Directions:
1. Preheat oven to 350°F.
2. Combine ingredients.
3. Form cookies and bake.

Nutritional Information: 70 calories, 2g protein, 14g carbohydrates, 1g fat

🐾 Beef & Veggie Medley

🍽 Yield: 2 servings | Prep time: 10 minutes | Cook time: 20 minutes

Age: 8+ months

Weight per Serving: 50g

Ingredients:
- 1/2 cup cooked beef, minced
- 1/4 cup peas
- 1/4 cup carrots, diced

Directions:
1. Mix ingredients.
2. Serve as a treat.

Nutritional Information: 110 calories, 8g protein, 7g carbohydrates, 5g fat

 **Peanut Crunch Bars**

Yield: 4 servings | Prep time: 10 minutes | Cook time: 15 minutes

Age: 6+ months

Weight per Serving: 25g

Ingredients:
- 1/2 cup peanuts, crushed
- 1 cup oat flour

Directions:
1. Preheat oven to 350°F.
2. Mix ingredients and press into a tray.
3. Bake and cut into bars.

Nutritional Information: 110 calories, 5g protein, 12g carbohydrates, 6g fat

 **Salmon Squares**

Yield: 6 servings | Prep time: 10 minutes | Cook time: 12 minutes

Age: 8+ months

Weight per Serving: 20g

Ingredients:
- 1/2 cup cooked salmon, flaked
- 1 cup whole wheat flour

Directions:
1. Preheat oven to 350°F.
2. Mix ingredients and press into a tray.
3. Bake and cut into squares.

Nutritional Information: 80 calories, 5g protein, 14g carbohydrates, 1.5g fat

Cheese & Apple Balls

Yield: 4 servings | Prep time: 10 minutes | Cook time: 15 minutes

Age: 6+ months

Weight per Serving: 20g

Ingredients:
- 1/2 cup grated cheese
- 1 apple, grated

Directions:
1. Preheat oven to 350°F.
2. Mix ingredients and roll into balls.
3. Bake until golden.

Nutritional Information: 85 calories, 4g protein, 10g carbohydrates, 4g fat

Tuna & Parsley Bites

Yield: 4 servings | Prep time: 10 minutes | Cook time: 15 minutes

Age: 6+ months

Weight per Serving: 20g

Ingredients:
- 1 can of tuna in water, drained
- 1 tbsp fresh parsley, chopped
- 1/2 cup oat flour

Directions:
1. Preheat oven to 350°F.
2. Mix ingredients in a bowl.
3. Form into bite-sized patties and place on a baking sheet.
4. Bake until golden brown.

Nutritional Information: 70 calories, 7g protein, 8g carbohydrates, 1g fat

Veggie & Quinoa Puffs

Yield: 6 servings | Prep time: 15 minutes | Cook time: 20 minutes

Age: 7+ months

Weight per Serving: 25g

Ingredients:

- 1/2 cup cooked quinoa
- 1/4 cup peas
- 1/4 cup grated carrot
- 1 egg

Directions:

1. Preheat oven to 350°F.
2. Mix all ingredients in a bowl.
3. Spoon small mounds onto a baking sheet.
4. Bake until set and slightly golden.

Nutritional Information: 55 calories, 3g protein, 9g carbohydrates, 1g fat

Lamb & Mint Cookies

Yield: 4 servings | Prep time: 15 minutes | Cook time: 18 minutes

Age: 8+ months

Weight per Serving: 20g

Ingredients:

- 1/2 cup cooked lamb, minced
- 1 tbsp fresh mint, chopped
- 1 cup oat flour

Directions:

1. Preheat oven to 350°F.
2. Mix ingredients in a bowl.
3. Roll out and cut into desired shapes.
4. Bake until crispy.

Nutritional Information: 90 calories, 6g protein, 12g carbohydrates, 3g fat

Blueberry & Yogurt Drops

Yield: 2 servings | Prep time: 10 minutes | Cook time: 0 minutes

Age: 5+ months

Weight per Serving: 40g

Ingredients:

- 1/4 cup blueberries, mashed
- 1/2 cup plain yogurt

Directions:

1. Mix blueberries and yogurt.
2. Drop spoonfuls onto a tray lined with parchment paper.
3. Freeze until set.

Nutritional Information: 45 calories, 3g protein, 6g carbohydrates, 1g fat

Spinach & Cheese Muffins

Yield: 4 servings | Prep time: 10 minutes | Cook time: 18 minutes

Age: 7+ months

Weight per Serving: 30g

Ingredients:

- 1/2 cup spinach, finely chopped
- 1/4 cup grated cheese
- 1 egg
- 1/2 cup oat flour

Directions:

1. Preheat oven to 350°F.
2. Mix all ingredients in a bowl until combined.
3. Spoon mixture into mini muffin tins.
4. Bake until set and slightly golden.

Nutritional Information: 80 calories, 4g protein, 8g carbohydrates, 3g fat

Chicken & Rice Cakes

Yield: 4 servings | Prep time: 15 minutes | Cook time: 20 minutes

Age: 6+ months

Weight per Serving: 25g

Ingredients:
- 1/2 cup cooked chicken, minced
- 1/4 cup cooked rice
- 1 egg

Directions:
1. Preheat oven to 350°F.
2. Mix ingredients in a bowl.
3. Shape into small patties and place on a baking sheet.
4. Bake until golden brown.

Nutritional Information: 85 calories, 6g protein, 9g carbohydrates, 2g fat

Turkey & Cranberry Treats

Yield: 6 servings | Prep time: 15 minutes | Cook time: 15 minutes

Age: 7+ months

Weight per Serving: 20g

Ingredients:
- 1/2 cup cooked turkey, minced
- 1/4 cup dried cranberries, chopped (ensure no added sugars or flavorings)
- 1 cup whole wheat flour

Directions:
1. Preheat oven to 350°F.
2. Mix ingredients in a bowl.
3. Roll out and cut into desired shapes.
4. Bake until crispy.

Nutritional Information: 80 calories, 5g protein, 12g carbohydrates, 1.5g fat

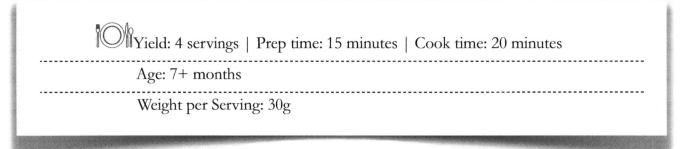

Broccoli & Beef Nuggets

Yield: 4 servings | Prep time: 15 minutes | Cook time: 20 minutes

Age: 7+ months

Weight per Serving: 30g

Ingredients:

- 1/2 cup cooked beef, minced
- 1/4 cup broccoli, finely chopped
- 1 egg

Directions:

1. Preheat oven to 350°F.
2. Mix all ingredients in a bowl.
3. Shape into nuggets and place on a baking sheet.
4. Bake until golden brown.

Nutritional Information: 100 calories, 7g protein, 5g carbohydrates, 5g fat

Quinoa & Carrot Sticks

Yield: 6 servings | Prep time: 15 minutes | Cook time: 20 minutes

Age: 7+ months

Weight per Serving: 25g

Ingredients:

- 1/2 cup cooked quinoa
- 1/4 cup grated carrot
- 1 egg

Directions:

1. Preheat oven to 350°F.
2. Mix all ingredients in a bowl.
3. Shape into sticks and place on a baking sheet.
4. Bake until crispy.

Nutritional Information: 60 calories, 3g protein, 8g carbohydrates, 1g fat

7.2 Dehydrated and jerky treats

Peanut & Honey Jerky

Yield: 5 servings | Prep time: 10 minutes | Cook time: 3 hours
- -
Age: 8+ months
- -
Weight per Serving: 30g

Ingredients:
- 1/2 cup unsalted peanuts, finely ground
- 1 tbsp honey

Directions:
1. Preheat oven to 200°F.
2. Mix ground peanuts and honey in a bowl.
3. Spread mixture thinly on a baking sheet.
4. Bake for 3 hours or until dried.
5. Cool and cut into strips.

Nutritional Information: 60 calories, 3g protein, 5g carbohydrates, 4g fat

Peanut Butter Banana Jerky

Yield: 4 servings | Prep time: 10 minutes | Cook time: 3 hours
- -
Age: 8+ months
- -
Weight per Serving: 30g

Ingredients:
- 2 ripe bananas
- 2 tbsp peanut butter (make sure it doesn't contain xylitol)

Directions:
1. Preheat oven to 200°F.
2. Mash bananas and mix with peanut butter.
3. Spread mixture thinly on a baking sheet.
4. Bake for 3 hours or until dried.
5. Cool and cut into strips.

Nutritional Information: 45 calories, 2g protein, 10g carbohydrates, 1.5g fat

# Beefy Bites

Yield: 5 servings | Prep time: 15 minutes | Cook time: 3 hours

Age: 9+ months

Weight per Serving: 35g

Ingredients:
- 1/2 lb lean beef, thinly sliced
- 1 tbsp parsley, finely chopped

Directions:
1. Preheat oven to 180°F.
2. Mix beef slices with parsley.
3. Place beef on a baking sheet.
4. Bake for 3 hours or until dehydrated.
5. Allow to cool.

Nutritional Information: 50 calories, 8g protein, 0g carbohydrates, 2g fat

# Dehydrated Veggie Medley

Yield: 5 servings | Prep time: 15 minutes | Cook time: 5 hours

Age: 7+ months

Weight per Serving: 30g

Ingredients:
- 1 carrot, thinly sliced
- 1 zucchini, thinly sliced
- 1 sweet potato, thinly sliced

Directions:
1. Preheat oven to 200°F.
2. Spread vegetable slices on a baking sheet.
3. Bake for 5 hours or until dried.
4. Allow to cool before serving.

Nutritional Information: 40 calories, 1g protein, 9g carbohydrates, 0.2g fat

 **Chicken & Parsley Chews**

🍽️ Yield: 6 servings | Prep time: 10 minutes | Cook time: 2 hours

Age: 8+ months

Weight per Serving: 40g

Ingredients:

- 2 boneless, skinless chicken breasts, thinly sliced
- 2 tbsp parsley, finely chopped

Directions:

1. Preheat oven to 180°F.
2. Coat chicken slices with parsley.
3. Place on a baking sheet.
4. Bake for 2 hours or until dehydrated.
5. Allow to cool before serving.

Nutritional Information: 60 calories, 14g protein, 0g carbohydrates, 1g fat

 **Salmon Slivers**

🍽️ Yield: 5 servings | Prep time: 10 minutes | Cook time: 2 hours

Age: 10+ months

Weight per Serving: 35g

Ingredients:

- 1/2 lb salmon fillet, skin removed
- 1 tbsp olive oil
- 1 tsp dried rosemary

Directions:

1. Preheat oven to 180°F.
2. Slice salmon into thin strips.
3. Toss with olive oil and rosemary.
4. Place on a baking sheet.
5. Bake for 2 hours or until dehydrated.
6. Allow to cool.

Nutritional Information: 70 calories, 8g protein, 0g carbohydrates, 4g fat

 # Oat & Apple Crunchies

Yield: 5 servings | Prep time: 15 minutes | Cook time: 2.5 hours

Age: 6+ months

Weight per Serving: 30g

Ingredients:
- 1 apple, grated
- 1 cup rolled oats
- 1/2 tsp cinnamon

Directions:
1. Preheat oven to 250°F.
2. Mix all ingredients in a bowl.
3. Shape into small bites and place on a baking sheet.
4. Bake for 2.5 hours.
5. Let cool and store in an airtight container.

Nutritional Information: 45 calories, 1g protein, 9g carbohydrates, 0.5g fat

 # Turmeric & Chicken Jerky

Yield: 4 servings | Prep time: 10 minutes | Cook time: 2 hours

Age: 8+ months

Weight per Serving: 40g

Ingredients:
- 2 boneless, skinless chicken breasts
- 1 tsp turmeric powder

Directions:
1. Preheat oven to 180°F.
2. Coat chicken slices with turmeric.
3. Place on a baking sheet.
4. Bake for 2 hours or until dehydrated.
5. Allow to cool.

Nutritional Information: 65 calories, 15g protein, 0g carbohydrates, 1g fat

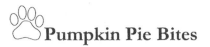
Pumpkin Pie Bites

Yield: 6 servings | Prep time: 15 minutes | Cook time: 2 hours

Age: 7+ months

Weight per Serving: 25g

Ingredients:
- 1/2 cup pure pumpkin puree
- 1/4 cup oat flour
- 1 tsp cinnamon

Directions:
1. Preheat oven to 250°F.
2. Mix all ingredients in a bowl.
3. Shape into small bites and place on a baking sheet.
4. Bake for 2 hours.
5. Let cool.

Nutritional Information: 30 calories, 1g protein, 6g carbohydrates, 0.3g fat

Tuna Flakes

Yield: 4 servings | Prep time: 10 minutes | Cook time: 3 hours

Age: 9+ months

Weight per Serving: 35g

Ingredients:
- 1 can of tuna in water, drained
- 1 tbsp parsley, finely chopped

Directions:
1. Preheat oven to 180°F.
2. Spread tuna flakes on a baking sheet.
3. Sprinkle with parsley.
4. Bake for 3 hours or until crispy.
5. Allow to cool before serving.

Nutritional Information: 50 calories, 11g protein, 0g carbohydrates, 1g fat

 **Coconut & Blueberry Bliss**

Yield: 5 servings | Prep time: 10 minutes | Cook time: 2 hours

Age: 8+ months

Weight per Serving: 25g

Ingredients:

- 1/2 cup unsweetened shredded coconut
- 1/4 cup fresh blueberries

Directions:

1. Preheat oven to 200°F.
2. Mix coconut and blueberries in a bowl.
3. Spread mixture thinly on a baking sheet.
4. Bake for 2 hours.
5. Allow to cool and break into pieces.

Nutritional Information: 40 calories, 0.5g protein, 3g carbohydrates, 3g fat

 **Turkey & Cranberry Jerky**

Yield: 5 servings | Prep time: 15 minutes | Cook time: 2 hours

Age: 10+ months

Weight per Serving: 40g

Ingredients:

- 1/2 lb lean turkey breast, thinly sliced
- 2 tbsp dried cranberries, finely chopped

Directions:

1. Preheat oven to 180°F.
2. Mix turkey slices with cranberries.
3. Place on a baking sheet.
4. Bake for 2 hours or until dehydrated.
5. Allow to cool.

Nutritional Information: 55 calories, 13g protein, 2g carbohydrates, 1g fat

Beet & Carrot Twists

Yield: 6 servings | Prep time: 20 minutes | Cook time: 3 hours

Age: 6+ months

Weight per Serving: 30g

Ingredients:
- 1 beet, peeled and thinly sliced
- 1 carrot, peeled and thinly sliced

Directions:
1. Preheat oven to 200°F.
2. Twist beet and carrot slices together.
3. Place on a baking sheet.
4. Bake for 3 hours or until dehydrated.
5. Allow to cool before serving.

Nutritional Information: 25 calories, 0.5g protein, 6g carbohydrates, 0.1g fat

Berry Delight Chewy Strips

Yield: 4 servings | Prep time: 10 minutes | Cook time: 3 hours

Age: 7+ months

Weight per Serving: 30g

Ingredients:
- 1 cup mixed berries (blueberries, strawberries, raspberries)
- 1 tbsp honey

Directions:
1. Preheat oven to 200°F.
2. Mash berries in a bowl and mix with honey.
3. Spread mixture thinly on a baking sheet.
4. Bake for 3 hours or until dried.
5. Cool and cut into strips.

Nutritional Information: 40 calories, 0.5g protein, 10g carbohydrates, 0.2g fat

7.3 Cold treats for hot days

Peanut Butter & Banana Popsicles

🍽 Yield: 4 servings | Prep time: 10 minutes | Freeze time: 4 hours

----

Age: Suitable for dogs aged 6 months and above

Weight per Serving: For dogs weighing 20-30 lbs

Ingredients:
- 2 ripe bananas
- 1/2 cup natural peanut butter
- 1/4 cup plain Greek yogurt

Directions:
1. Blend bananas, peanut butter, and yogurt until smooth.
2. Pour mixture into silicone molds or an ice cube tray.
3. Freeze for at least 4 hours.

Nutritional Info (approx. per serving): 190 calories, 7g protein, 25g carbohydrates, 8g fat

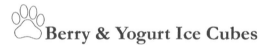Berry & Yogurt Ice Cubes

🍽 Yield: 6 servings | Prep time: 10 minutes | Freeze time: 3 hours

----

Age: Suitable for dogs aged 7 months and above

Weight per Serving: For dogs weighing 15-25 lbs

Ingredients:
- 1/2 cup blueberries
- 1/2 cup strawberries
- 1 cup plain Greek yogurt

Directions:
1. Blend berries and yogurt until smooth.
2. Pour mixture into silicone molds or an ice cube tray.
3. Freeze for at least 3 hours.

Nutritional Info (approx. per serving): 60 calories, 4g protein, 9g carbohydrates, 1g fat

Coconut & Pineapple Chunks

🍽 Yield: 4 servings | Prep time: 15 minutes | Freeze time: 4 hours

Age: Suitable for dogs aged 8 months and above

Weight per Serving: For dogs weighing 25-35 lbs

Ingredients:

- 1 cup pineapple chunks
- 1/2 cup coconut milk

Directions:

1. Blend pineapple and coconut milk until smooth.
2. Pour mixture into silicone molds or an ice cube tray.
3. Freeze for at least 4 hours.

Nutritional Info (approx. per serving): 120 calories, 2g protein, 18g carbohydrates, 6g fat

Apple & Carrot Slush

🍽 Yield: 5 servings | Prep time: 10 minutes | Freeze time: 3 hours

Age: Suitable for dogs aged 6 months and above

Weight per Serving: For dogs weighing 20-28 lbs

Ingredients:

- 1 apple, peeled and cored
- 2 carrots, peeled
- 1 cup water

Directions:

1. Blend apple, carrots, and water until smooth.
2. Pour mixture into silicone molds or an ice cube tray.
3. Freeze for at least 3 hours.

Nutritional Info (approx. per serving): 40 calories, 0.5g protein, 10g carbohydrates, 0.2g fat

Minty Fresh Breath Cubes

Yield: 6 servings | Prep time: 10 minutes | Freeze time: 2 hours

Age: Suitable for dogs aged 7 months and above

Weight per Serving: For dogs weighing 15-23 lbs

Ingredients:

- 1 cup fresh mint leaves
- 1/2 cucumber
- 1 cup water

Directions:

1. Blend mint leaves, cucumber, and water until smooth.
2. Pour mixture into silicone molds or an ice cube tray.
3. Freeze for at least 2 hours.

Nutritional Info (approx. per serving): 10 calories, 0.3g protein, 2g carbohydrates, 0.1g fat

Watermelon & Coconut Coolers

Yield: 4 servings | Prep time: 10 minutes | Freeze time: 3 hours

Age: Suitable for dogs aged 6 months and above

Weight per Serving: For dogs weighing 25-35 lbs

Ingredients:

- 2 cups watermelon chunks, seedless
- 1/2 cup coconut water

Directions:

1. Blend watermelon chunks and coconut water until smooth.
2. Pour mixture into silicone molds or an ice cube tray.
3. Freeze for at least 3 hours.

Nutritional Info (approx. per serving): 45 calories, 1g protein, 11g carbohydrates, 0.2g fat

Mango & Ginger Freeze

🍽 Yield: 5 servings | Prep time: 10 minutes | Freeze time: 4 hours

Age: Suitable for dogs aged 8 months and above

Weight per Serving: For dogs weighing 20-30 lbs

Ingredients:
- 1 ripe mango, peeled and pitted
- 1/2 tsp grated ginger
- 1 cup plain Greek yogurt

Directions:
1. Blend mango, ginger, and yogurt until smooth.
2. Pour mixture into silicone molds or an ice cube tray.
3. Freeze for at least 4 hours.

Nutritional Info (approx. per serving): 70 calories, 4g protein, 12g carbohydrates, 1g fat

Peanut & Honey Drops

🍽 Yield: 6 servings | Prep time: 10 minutes | Freeze time: 2 hours

Age: Suitable for dogs aged 7 months and above

Weight per Serving: For dogs weighing 18-26 lbs

Ingredients:
- 1/2 cup natural peanut butter
- 2 tbsp honey
- 1/2 cup water

Directions:
1. Blend peanut butter, honey, and water until smooth.
2. Pour mixture into silicone molds or an ice cube tray.
3. Freeze for at least 2 hours.

Nutritional Info (approx. per serving): 130 calories, 5g protein, 9g carbohydrates, 9g fat

Berry & Chia Pops

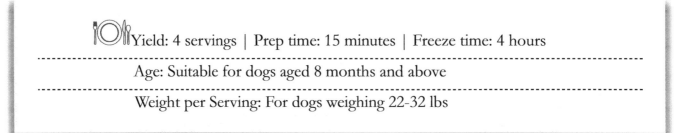

Yield: 4 servings | Prep time: 15 minutes | Freeze time: 4 hours

Age: Suitable for dogs aged 8 months and above

Weight per Serving: For dogs weighing 22-32 lbs

Ingredients:

- 1 cup mixed berries (blueberries, strawberries, raspberries)
- 1 tbsp chia seeds
- 1 cup coconut milk

Directions:

1. Blend berries and coconut milk until smooth.
2. Mix in chia seeds.
3. Pour mixture into silicone molds or an ice cube tray.
4. Freeze for at least 4 hours.

Nutritional Info (approx. per serving): 120 calories, 3g protein, 13g carbohydrates, 7g fat

Green Tea & Apple Cubes

Yield: 6servings | Prep time: 10 minutes | Freeze time: 3 hours

Age: Suitable for dogs aged 9 months and above

Weight per Serving: For dogs weighing 20-28 lbs

Ingredients:

- 1 green tea bag
- 1 cup hot water
- 1 apple, peeled, cored, and chopped

Directions:

1. Brew green tea in hot water and let it cool.
2. Blend the cooled tea and apple chunks until smooth.
3. Pour mixture into silicone molds or an ice cube tray.
4. Freeze for at least 3 hours.

Nutritional Info (approx. per serving): 30 calories, 0.4g protein, 8g carbohydrates, 0.1g fat

7.4 Chewy delights

Sweet Potato Chews

Yield: 4 servings | Prep time: 10 minutes | Cook time: 2-3 hours

Age: Suitable for dogs aged 6 months and above

Weight per Serving: For dogs weighing 20-30 lbs

Ingredients:
- 2 large sweet potatoes

Directions:
1. Preheat oven to 250°F.
2. Slice sweet potatoes into 1/4-inch thick rounds.
3. Place slices on a baking sheet lined with parchment paper.
4. Bake for 2-3 hours, turning occasionally, until chewy.

Nutritional Info (approx. per serving): 110 calories, 2g protein, 26g carbohydrates, 0.2g fat

Peanut Butter & Oat Bars

Yield: 6 servings | Prep time: 15 minutes | Cook time: 20 minutes

Age: Suitable for dogs aged 8 months and above

Weight per Serving: For dogs weighing 25-35 lbs

Ingredients:
- 2 cups rolled oats
- 1 cup natural peanut butter
- 1/4 cup honey

Directions:
1. Preheat oven to 350°F.
2. Combine all ingredients in a mixing bowl.
3. Press mixture into a baking dish.
4. Bake for 20 minutes.
5. Let cool and cut into bars.

Nutritional Info (approx. per serving): 260 calories, 10g protein, 30g carbohydrates, 14g fat

Chicken Jerky Strips

Yield: 4 servings | Prep time: 10 minutes | Cook time: 2 hours

Age: Suitable for dogs aged 7 months and above

Weight per Serving: For dogs weighing 20-30 lbs

Ingredients:
- 2 boneless chicken breasts

Directions:
1. Preheat oven to 200°F.
2. Slice chicken breasts into thin strips.
3. Place on a baking sheet lined with parchment paper.
4. Bake for 2 hours or until chewy.
5. Store in an airtight container.

Nutritional Info (approx. per serving): 130 calories, 30g protein, 0g carbohydrates, 1g fat

Beef & Carrot Sticks

Yield: 5 servings | Prep time: 15 minutes | Cook time: 30 minutes

Age: Suitable for dogs aged 9 months and above

Weight per Serving: For dogs weighing 25-35 lbs

Ingredients:
- 1/2 lb ground beef
- 1 cup grated carrots
- 1/4 cup whole wheat flour

Directions:
1. Preheat oven to 375°F.
2. Mix all ingredients together.
3. Shape into stick forms and place on a baking sheet.
4. Bake for 30 minutes.

Nutritional Info (approx. per serving): 160 calories, 14g protein, 10g carbohydrates, 7g fat

Salmon & Parsley Bites

Yield: 6 servings | Prep time: 20 minutes | Cook time: 25 minutes

Age: Suitable for dogs aged 10 months and above

Weight per Serving: For dogs weighing 20-30 lbs

Ingredients:

- 1/2 lb cooked salmon, flaked
- 1/4 cup chopped parsley
- 1 egg
- 1 cup oat flour

Directions:

1. Preheat oven to 375°F.
2. Mix all ingredients together.
3. Shape into small bites and place on a baking sheet.
4. Bake for 25 minutes.

Nutritional Info (approx. per serving): 170 calories, 15g protein, 12g carbohydrates, 7g fat

Apple & Cinnamon Rolls

Yield: 4 servings | Prep time: 20 minutes | Cook time: 30 minutes

Age: Suitable for dogs aged 7 months and above

Weight per Serving: For dogs weighing 18-25 lbs

Ingredients:

- 1 apple, peeled, cored, and finely chopped
- 1/2 tsp cinnamon
- 1 cup oat flour
- 1/4 cup water

Directions:

1. Preheat oven to 350°F.
2. Mix chopped apple, cinnamon, oat flour, and water in a bowl.
3. Roll the mixture into small rolls and place on a lined baking sheet.
4. Bake for 30 minutes until chewy.

Nutritional Info (approx. per serving): 110 calories, 3g protein, 25g carbohydrates, 1g fat

🐾 Banana & Coconut Chewies

Yield: 5 servings | **Prep time:** 15 minutes | **Cook time:** 25 minutes

Age: Suitable for dogs aged 8 months and above

Weight per Serving: For dogs weighing 20-28 lbs

Ingredients:

- 1 ripe banana, mashed
- 1/2 cup shredded coconut
- 1 cup oat flour

Directions:

1. Preheat oven to 350°F.
2. Mix mashed banana, shredded coconut, and oat flour in a bowl.
3. Shape the mixture into small cookies and place on a lined baking sheet.
4. Bake for 25 minutes until chewy.

Nutritional Info (approx. per serving): 145 calories, 4g protein, 20g carbohydrates, 6g fat

🐾 Blueberry & Almond Bars

Yield: 6 servings | **Prep time:** 20 minutes | **Cook time:** 25 minutes

Age: Suitable for dogs aged 10 months and above

Weight per Serving: For dogs weighing 25-35 lbs

Ingredients:

- 1/2 cup fresh blueberries
- 1/2 cup almond butter
- 1 cup whole wheat flour

Directions:

1. Preheat oven to 350°F.
2. Mix blueberries, almond butter, and whole wheat flour in a bowl.
3. Press the mixture into a baking dish.
4. Bake for 25 minutes.
5. Allow to cool and cut into bars.

Nutritional Info (approx. per serving): 220 calories, 7g protein, 24g carbohydrates, 12g fat

Pumpkin & Flaxseed Twists

Yield: 4 servings | **Prep time:** 20 minutes | **Cook time:** 30 minutes

Age: Suitable for dogs aged 8 months and above

Weight per Serving: For dogs weighing 20-28 lbs

Ingredients:
- 1/2 cup pumpkin puree
- 1/4 cup ground flaxseed
- 1 cup oat flour

Directions:
1. Preheat oven to 350°F.
2. Mix pumpkin puree, ground flaxseed, and oat flour in a bowl.
3. Roll the mixture into small twists and place on a lined baking sheet.
4. Bake for 30 minutes until chewy.

Nutritional Info (approx. per serving): 135 calories, 5g protein, 20g carbohydrates, 5g fat

Spinach & Carrot Sticks

Yield: 5 servings | **Prep time:** 15 minutes | **Cook time:** 30 minutes

Age: Suitable for dogs aged 9 months and above

Weight per Serving: For dogs weighing 22-32 lbs

Ingredients:
- 1/2 cup finely chopped spinach
- 1/2 cup grated carrots
- 1 cup whole wheat flour
- 1/4 cup water

Directions:
1. Preheat oven to 350°F.
2. Combine spinach, carrots, whole wheat flour, and water in a bowl.
3. Shape mixture into stick forms and place on a baking sheet.
4. Bake for 30 minutes until chewy.

Nutritional Info (approx. per serving): 120 calories, 4g protein, 25g carbohydrates, 1g fat

Chapter 8: The Importance of Hydration

Just as with humans, water is a critical component of a dog's body, making up a significant percentage of their total body weight. Ensuring your dog is adequately hydrated is crucial for a host of bodily functions, from temperature regulation to digestion.

8.1 Understanding Dogs' Hydration Needs Across Seasons

- Spring & Summer:
  - These warmer months mean increased temperatures and often more outdoor activity. Dogs will require more water as they're more prone to panting and increased metabolic rates.
  - Always ensure water bowls are filled, especially after exercise.
  - Beware of hot pavements and direct sun exposure which can increase dehydration risks.
- Autumn & Winter:
  - Although cooler, indoor heating can cause dehydration.
  - Snow is not a sufficient water substitute; ensure regular access to liquid water.
  - Despite reduced activity, water remains crucial for metabolic processes.

8.2 Flavorful Broth Recipes for Hydration

Chicken & Carrot Broth

Yield: 7 cups | Prep time: 10 minutes | Cook time: 40 minutes

Age: Suitable for dogs aged 7 months and above

Weight per Serving: Depends on the dog's size and dietary needs

Ingredients:
- 2 chicken breasts
- 3 carrots, sliced
- 6 cups of water

Directions:
1. Place all ingredients in a pot.
2. Simmer until the chicken is cooked through.
3. Strain and cool before serving. Store in the refrigerator.

Nutritional Info (approx. per serving 1 cup): 70 calories, 10g protein, 5g carbohydrates, 1g fat

Vegetable Hydration Broth

Yield: 6 cups | Prep time: 10 minutes | Cook time: 20 minutes

Age: Suitable for dogs aged 7 months and above

Weight per Serving: Depends on the dog's size and dietary needs

Ingredients:
- 1 cup of chopped spinach
- 1/2 cup of chopped pumpkin
- 5 cups of water

Directions:
1. Combine ingredients in a pot.
2. Bring to a boil, then simmer for 20 minutes.
3. Strain and cool. Store any extras in the refrigerator.

Nutritional Info (approx. per serving 1 cup): 20 calories, 1g protein, 4g carbohydrates, 0.2g fat

Beef & Parsley Broth

Yield: 7 cups | Prep time: 10 minutes | Cook time: 3 hours

Age: Suitable for dogs aged 7 months and above

Weight per Serving: Depends on the dog's size and dietary needs

Ingredients:
- 2 beef marrow bones
- A handful of fresh parsley (cleanses the kidneys)
- 6 cups of water

Directions:
1. Place beef bones and parsley in a large pot.
2. Cover with water.
3. Bring to a simmer and let it cook for about 3 hours.
4. Strain the broth and let it cool. Store in the refrigerator for up to 5 days.

Nutritional Info (approx. per serving 1 cup): 80 calories, 12g protein, 1g carbohydrates, 3g fat

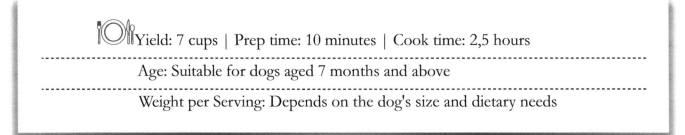

Turkey & Sweet Potato Broth

Yield: 7 cups | Prep time: 10 minutes | Cook time: 2,5 hours

Age: Suitable for dogs aged 7 months and above

Weight per Serving: Depends on the dog's size and dietary needs

Ingredients:

- 2 turkey necks
- 1 medium sweet potato, diced
- 6 cups of water

Directions:

1. Combine turkey necks and sweet potato in a pot.
2. Fill with water.
3. Simmer for 2.5 hours, ensuring the turkey cooks thoroughly.
4. Strain the broth, discarding the solids. Once cooled, refrigerate.

Nutritional Info (approx. per serving 1 cup): 90 calories, 11g protein, 7g carbohydrates, 2g fat

Fish & Pea Broth

Yield: 7 cups | Prep time: 15 minutes | Cook time: 1,5 hours

Age: Suitable for dogs aged 7 months and above

Weight per Serving: Depends on the dog's size and dietary needs

Ingredients:

- 2 whole mackerels or sardines (gutted and cleaned)
- 1 cup of fresh or frozen peas
- 6 cups of water

Directions:

1. Put the fish and peas into a pot.
2. Cover with water.
3. Simmer for about 1.5 hours.
4. Strain the liquid and let it cool. Refrigerate the broth.

Nutritional Info (approx. per serving 1 cup): 60 calories, 9g protein, 5g carbohydrates, 2g fat

8.3 Tips on Ensuring Your Dog is Drinking Enough

- Fresh & Clean: Regularly refill and clean water bowls to ensure a fresh supply.
- Multiple Bowls: If you have a large house or yard, consider placing multiple water bowls in different locations.
- Hydration Indicators: Monitor your dog's urine. If it's dark yellow or has a strong odor, they might not be drinking enough. Clear to light yellow is generally indicative of proper hydration.
- Wet Food: If your dog eats dry kibble, occasionally mixing in some wet food can increase their water intake.
- Ice Cubes: Some dogs love playing with and munching on ice cubes, a great way to supplement their water intake in warm weather.
- Regular Checks: Lift the skin between your dog's shoulder blades; it should spring

Chapter 9: The Importance of Gradual Transitions

Switching to homemade dog food isn't an overnight affair. It's a journey, and like all journeys, it's best taken step by step. Dogs, being creatures of habit, might resist abrupt changes in their diet. Here's a methodical approach:

- Week 1: Introduce homemade food as a treat. Let your dog get used to the taste without making it a primary meal component.
- Week 2: Replace about a quarter of their commercial food with the homemade version. Observe for any adverse reactions.
- Week 3: Now, homemade food can form half of their meal. By now, they should be more accustomed to the taste and texture.
- Week 4: Increase the proportion to three-quarters. Monitor their energy levels and overall health.
- Week 5: Your dog should now be ready for a full homemade meal.

Remember, always maintain hydration and ensure that the homemade food covers all nutritional bases. It might be beneficial to consult a veterinarian or a pet nutritionist during this transition.

Steps for a Smooth Dietary Transition

Research and Planning
- Consulting with a veterinarian or canine nutritionist
- Creating a week-by-week plan

Introducing New Foods Slowly
- The 25-75 rule for new and old food mix
- Monitoring your dog's reactions and adjusting accordingly

Paying Attention to Portion Sizes
- Adjusting quantities based on caloric needs and weight goals
- Using measuring tools for consistency

Maintaining Hydration
- Ensuring water intake remains consistent or increases with diet changes
- Using broths to entice drinking when introducing drier foods

Chapter 10: 28-Day Transition Meal Plan

This chapter offers a comprehensive, day-by-day breakdown for a 28-day period. The goal is to seamlessly integrate homemade meals into your dog's diet while ensuring their comfort and health.

Week 1: The Gentle Introduction

- Day 1 to 3:
  - ✓ Breakfast:
    - Store-bought food (3/4 of the portion)
    - Chicken and rice blend: Boiled chicken (shredded) mixed with cooked rice (1/4 of the portion).
  - ✓ Dinner:
    - Store-bought food (3/4 of the portion)
    - Vegetable puree: Blend steamed carrots, peas, and sweet potato (1/4 of the portion).
- Day 4 to 7:
  - ✓ Breakfast:
    - Store-bought food (2/3 of the portion)
    - Beef and quinoa mix: Ground beef cooked in minimal oil combined with cooked quinoa (1/3 of the portion).
  - ✓ Dinner:
    - Store-bought food (2/3 of the portion)
    - Vegetable and chicken broth: Homemade chicken broth mixed with finely chopped veggies (1/3 of the portion).

Week 2: Balancing Act

- Day 8 to 10:
  - ✓ Breakfast:
    - Store-bought food (1/2 of the portion)
    - Turkey and barley stew: Slow-cooked turkey pieces with barley and a dash of turmeric (1/2 of the portion).
  - ✓ Dinner:
    - Store-bought food (1/2 of the portion)
    - Fish and greens: Steamed mackerel mixed with spinach and zucchini (1/2 of the portion).
- Day 11 to 14:
  - ✓ Breakfast:
    - Store-bought food (1/2 of the portion)
    - Pork and vegetable blend: Lean pork pieces cooked with bell peppers, broccoli, and peas (1/2 of the portion).
  - ✓ Dinner:
    - Store-bought food (1/2 of the portion)
    - Egg and sweet potato scramble: Scrambled eggs mixed with mashed sweet potato and a sprinkle of chia seeds (1/2 of the portion).

Week 3: Tipping the Scales

- Day 15 to 18:
  - ✓ Breakfast:
    - Store-bought food (1/4 of the portion)
    - Lamb and carrot stew: Slow-cooked lamb chunks with carrots, flavored with rosemary (3/4 of the portion).
  - ✓ Dinner:
    - Store-bought food (1/4 of the portion)
    - Chicken liver and rice: Lightly sautéed chicken liver mixed with cooked rice (3/4 of the portion).
- Day 19 to 21:
  - ✓ Breakfast:
    - Store-bought food (1/4 of the portion)
    - Beef and pumpkin mash: Ground beef with mashed pumpkin and a sprinkle of flax seeds (3/4 of the portion).
  - ✓ Dinner:
    - Store-bought food (1/4 of the portion)
    - Fish broth and quinoa: Fish broth (sardine or mackerel based) combined with cooked quinoa (3/4 of the portion).

Week 4: The Complete Transition

- Day 22 to 28:
  - ✓ Breakfast:
    - Chicken, blueberries, and spinach scramble: Shredded boiled chicken, a handful of blueberries, and wilted spinach. Optionally, add a small spoon of coconut oil for added fats.
  - ✓ Dinner:
    - Pork, apple, and broccoli stir-fry: Diced pork pieces stir-fried with apple slices and broccoli florets in a minimal amount of olive oil.

Monitoring:
- Digestive Comfort: This should be the primary concern. Note any change in your dog's bowel movements. A bit of inconsistency in the beginning is normal, but prolonged diarrhea or constipation requires a vet's attention.
- Energy Levels: A balanced meal should not make your dog lethargic. If your dog seems less energetic than usual, review the recipes to ensure they are getting a balanced diet.
- Skin and Coat: A healthy diet often reflects in a dog's coat. If you notice excessive shedding or dry skin, it could be an indicator of allergies or missing nutrients.

Conclusion

As we close the pages of the "Homemade Healthy Dog Food Cookbook: Make Your Furry Friend Live Healthier & Longer with 130 Easy and Scrumptious Recipes for a Balanced Diet, Healthy Treats, and 28-Day Transition Meal Plan," it's my hope that you feel empowered and inspired. Preparing meals for our furry friends is more than just a culinary endeavor; it's a declaration of love. Through the 130 recipes provided, the aim was to ensure your pet not only relishes their meals but also thrives on them. The journey towards a balanced diet doesn't just end here; it's a continuous path of discovery as you learn more about your pet's preferences and nutritional needs.

The 28-Day Transition Meal Plan serves as a guide for those new to homemade dog meals. Remember, it's natural for dogs to experience minor adjustments, but always be vigilant and consult your veterinarian if in doubt.

In a world of commercial dog foods, taking the time to prepare meals at home signifies a commitment to the well-being and happiness of our pets. It's our chance to give back to the loyal companions who bring endless joy and unconditional love into our lives. You've equipped yourself with the knowledge to provide nutritionally sound, balanced meals for your canine family member.

May this cookbook be a constant companion in your kitchen, guiding you as you craft delicious, wholesome meals, ensuring a healthier, longer, and happier life for your dog. Remember, it's not just about adding years to their life, but life to their years.

Here's to happy tails and contented woofs!
Cheers to a journey of health.

Made in the USA
Las Vegas, NV
20 December 2023

83335821R10050